D1825434

Hodder & Stoughton *Publishers*

338 Euston Road
London
NW1 3BH
Tel: 071 873 6000

This book has been made available to you on approval. Once it is purchased, it may be photocopied for use within the purchasing institution only. Any photocopying prior to purchase is in breach of copyright.

If you do not wish to retain this book, please return it to the publishers. It will only be accepted by them, however, if the declaration below has been filled in and signed. Failure to do so will be taken to imply that the material has already been copied.

General Studies Resource Books

Political and Social Issues

0 340 59534 5

In returning this photocopiable book, which has been supplied to me on approval, I confirm that no copies have been made of any part of the publication.

Name   ....

Position   ....

Name and address of educational establishment:

....

....

....

....

....

• GENERAL STUDIES RESOURCE BOOKS •

POLITICAL AND SOCIAL ISSUES

Paul Higginson

Hodder & Stoughton

A MEMBER OF THE HODDER HEADLINE GROUP

Acknowledgements

The author would like to thank Carole Woodburn for typing the script.

The Publishers would like to thank the following for their kind permission to reproduce material: Central Statistics Office for information given on p79; Don McCullin for the photograph on p80; Sunday Times Newspapers for the material on p22f; UNISON for extracts on p39; also The Associated Examining Board, The Northern Examinations and Assessment Board and The University of Oxford, Delegacy of Local Examinations for use of examination questions from past papers. Please note that any answers, or hints of answers, to the questions from past papers on pages 95f are the responsibility of the author and have not been provided or approved by the Boards.

Every effort has been made to trace copyright holders of material reproduced in this book. The Publishers will be glad to make suitable arrangements with any copyright holders whom it has not been possible to contact.

For Sue

Cataloguing in Publication Data is available from the British Library

ISBN 0340 595345

First published 1994

Impression number   10 9 8 7 6 5 4 3 2 1

Year   1998 1997 1996 1995 1994

Copyright © 1994 Paul Higginson

Published by Hodder & Stoughton Educational, a division of Hodder Headline Plc. The Publishers grant permission for multiple copies of this sheet to be made in the place of purchase for use solely in that institution.

Printed in Great Britain for Hodder & Stoughton Educational, a division of Hodder Headline Plc, 338 Euston Road, London NW1 3BH by St Edmundsbury Press, Bury St Edmunds.

Contents

Introduction   4

Teacher's Notes   8

1 What is Politics?   15

2 Elections, Parties and Policies   20

3 Parliament and Government   26

4 Public Spending   31

5 Pressure Groups   37

6 The Law   44

7 Europe   51

8 The Media   57

9 Poverty   63

10 Gender   69

11 Race and Ethnic Minorities   77

12 Crime and Punishment   85

Additional Information   93

Introduction

General Studies Resource Books are designed for groups studying A-level and sixth form General Studies, but can also be used for BTEC Courses; Key Stage 4 Years 11 to 13 and tutor groups. Book One (Political and Social Issues) will also prove an invaluable resource for Politics, Citizenship and Social Science courses. Each unit is self-contained, with resource pages which can be photocopies or transferred to OHPs, and worksheets for classroom or homework use.

AIMS

This book aims to encourage students to:

1 think critically on significant political and social problems and issues in the modern world;

2 understand and evaluate a range of often conflicting arguments on each topic;

3 communicate information and viewpoints in a clear, analytical manner, supported by relevant evidence.

EXAMINATIONS

The 12 units have been designed to support a variety of courses. General Studies can be studied at A- and A/S-level. Courses are multi-disciplinary covering the major social, political, moral and environmental issues, as well as science and, in some cases, mathematics and a foreign language (see table on page 5). All examinations require good English and communication skills. The style and format of the final written papers vary but most boards include data response, short answer and comprehension questions (NEAB also includes multi-choice) and all examinations require candidates to write answers to essay questions. It is also possible to take a coursework option which enables students to submit an in-depth assignment on a selected topic. As syllabus details are constantly changing, students who are taking General Studies independently from their school or college should write to the examination boards to obtain an up-to-date syllabus and past paper questions. Units 1 to 8 and 12 will be useful to students following A-level and GCSE Politics courses and Units 1, 2, 5, 6, 8 to 12 cover key topics in Sociology. This book can also be used for teaching Education for Citizenship, one of the five cross-curricular themes identified by the National Curriculum Council.

Hodder & Stoughton

© 1994 Paul Higginson. The publishers grant permission for multiple copies of this sheet to be made in the place of purchase for use solely in that institution.

EXAMINATION BOARD DETAILS

Board	Address & Tel. No.	Coursework	Coursework Assessment	Examination Papers	Comments
Associated Examining Board (AEB)	Stag Hill House Guildford Surrey GU2 5XJ (0483) 506506	Compulsory: two assignments (2,500-3,000 words) on prescribed titles. (20% of examination.)	Internally assessed, externally moderated.	Paper 1: 2.5 hrs (30%) Paper 2: 3 hrs (50%)	Coursework topics are given by board in advance, e.g. for 1994 candidates choose two of four themes: Space, Communication, Conflict and Leisure.
University of Cambridge Local Examinations Syndicate	Syndicate Buildings 1 Hills Road Cambridge CB1 2EU (0223) 61111	Optional: 6,000 word study of own choice on a single issue, or a series of short related studies.	Internally assessed, externally moderated.	Paper 1: 3 hrs (50%) Paper 2: 1.5 hrs (25%) Paper 3: 1.5 hrs (25%)	A bonus mark is awarded for the coursework. This will not lower the overall grade but may improve it by one, or at most, two grades.
Northern Examinations and Assessment Board (NEAB)	Devas Street Manchester M15 6EU (061) 953 1180	Scheme 1: No coursework. Scheme 2: Personal study (or six assignments) on topic of own choice. Suggested length 4,000-7,000 words. (30% of examination)	Internally assessed.	Scheme 1 Paper 1: 3 hrs (50%) Paper 2: 3 hrs (50%) Scheme 2 Paper 1: 2.5 hrs (40%) Paper 2: 2 hrs (30%)	Candidates opting for coursework (Scheme 2) sit the same two papers as Scheme 1 students but do not answer any essay questions. (Scheme 1 students answer three essay questions.)
University of Oxford Delagacy of Local Examinations	Ewart House Summertown Oxford OX2 7BZ (0865) 54291			Paper 1: 3 hrs (50%) Paper 2: 3 hrs (50%)	The syllabus covers three main areas: the arts (visual, music, performing, verbal); the organisation of society (political, economic, social and moral issues); science and technology (matter, energy, scientific thought, environmental issues).

NEAB and Oxford have Mathematics/Numeracy Sections. NEAB has a foreign language section. All of the four boards require students to answer questions on Political and Social Issues, Moral and Environmental Issues, Science and Technology.

The boards listed above also offer A/S-level General Studies, along with London, Oxford & Cambridge, Wales and Northern Ireland.

Hodder & Stoughton

© 1994 Paul Higginson. The publishers grant permission for multiple copies of this sheet to be made in the place of purchase for use solely in that institution.

WRITING ESSAYS - TEN POINTS TO REMEMBER

1   Make a short plan jotting down key ideas, names and paragraph headings.

2   **The Introduction** - define the key words or phrases in the title, then briefly state the line or argument you intend to pursue in your essay. Tell the reader (the examiner) what you are going to write about, using the words of the title. This shows the examiner that you are answering the question set (not the question you would have liked to have been set!) and helps to keep your answer relevant.

3   **The Body** - argue your line, beginning with the most convincing point to support your argument. Remember that there will always be two or more sides to every question, so you must always deal with the counter-arguments. So, if the question asks 'Should the monarchy be abolished?' and your line is that it should, you must also deal with all the arguments which suggest that the monarchy is wonderful and should be retained.

4   Essays require a combination of evidence (information, facts, detail, statistics, examples, quotes, etc.,) and analysis (this is how you use the evidence to prove something or support a line). Therefore, essays should contain supporting evidence to back up each point. The single most common error in General Studies (and most Social Science) examination papers is the superficial and sweeping statement unsubstantiated by any facts or evidence.

5   Throughout the essay make sure you keep referring to the words of the title; relate everything you write to the question which has been set.

6   Keep your writing as academic as possible. Take care not to use slang, colloquialisms, clichés and generalisations. Avoid the phrase 'I think' - just say it! ('The monarchy should be abolished' and not 'I think the monarchy should be abolished'.)

7   Take care over how your work is presented. Examiners continually complain about poor handwriting (some scripts are illegible), spelling, grammar and punctuation.

8   Usually General Studies questions seek to be topical so use recent, contemporary examples to back up your arguments. Keep up to date with current events by reading quality newspapers and watching the news each day. However, avoid the temptation to write down everything you know about a particular topic without first checking that it is relevant to the question.

9   Make comparisons when appropriate with other fields of study, other countries, other period of history, etc. General Studies aims to encourage students to be inter-disciplinary and comparative. So compare our contemporary monarchy with other monarchies (e.g. Sweden, Spain) and republics (e.g. USA, France), and make reference to kings and queens in history.

10 **The conclusion** - avoid the tired old phrase 'In conclusion', again just say it. Re-state your line using the words of the title: this is a good double check that you have answered the question. Too many students play safe by writing 'on the one hand this... on the other hand that'. Be confident in your argument and briefly summarize the main points again in one sentence: 'The monarchy should be abolished because...'. Some students like to finish with a final contemporary example or apt quotation which effectively proves their line.

Hodder & Stoughton   © 1994 Paul Higginson. The publishers grant permission for multiple copies of this sheet to be made in the place of purchase for use solely in that institution.

EFFECTIVE STUDY

Follow these guidelines to improve your study technique.

1 The best way of broadening your knowledge and improving your written English, outside the class, is to read and make notes at home. (Teachers and examination boards can provide relevant reading lists.) Always jot down brief notes when you are reading, otherwise the material will soon be forgotten and you will have nothing to revise from.

2 Each issue or problem will always contain two or more sides or arguments. Do not ignore viewpoints you disagree with - try to understand them as effectively as possible.

3 Examiners have indicated that they require some acquaintance with articles in the quality press and 'serious' television programmes.

4 Develop your verbal skills by actively participating in class discussion and debate. Avoid the temptation to say the first thing that comes into your head and try to think out your point in advance and present it in a logical, coherent way.

5 Keep a diary of current events. Include facts, dates, arguments, personalities involved, statistics, etc. Cut relevant articles out of newspapers and journals.

6 Before you sit your examination look over the syllabus and past papers and answer questions under timed conditions. Work out in advance how much time you must spend on each section of the paper (look at the marks awarded for each question) and then stick to this in the examination.

Hodder & Stoughton
© 1994 Paul Higginson. The publishers grant permission for multiple copies of this sheet to be made in the place of purchase for use solely in that institution.

Teacher's Notes

This book can either be used as a complete course in itself or as a resource package to supplement the teacher's existing material. The units are flexible and can be taught in a variety of ways but the emphasis throughout is on active student participation through discussion, structured worksheets, simulations and group work. The aim is to get students to look beyond their specialist fields at important aspects of the modern world, broadening and deepening their knowledge, acquiring the skills to critically evaluate complex and often conflicting points of view.

Before working through the material in a unit each lesson should ideally begin with a short brainstorming session where students provide the teacher with all the information and ideas they already have on a particular topic - anything that is relevant should be placed on the board or OHP. This allows students to make an immediate contribution while enabling the teacher to check the group's knowledge, or lack of it, on a particular topic. When using the worksheets (for example, Writing a Constitution on p18) allow the students the time to think through the arguments for themselves before giving them the worksheet material. The notes below provide brief answers to questions or exercises where specific and detailed knowledge or information is required. Guidelines are also provided on how to get the best results from the simulations and role plays.

UNIT 1 - WHAT IS POLITICS?

Problem solving - Q.1: Possible solutions might include: a united Ireland, a separate independent Northern Irish state, devolution within the UK, greater integration into the rest of the UK, an autonomous region within a federal 'regionalised' Europe, placing Ulster under UN control, etc.

Worksheet 3 - Further Questions 2: You may like to develop this by examining other factors which determine voting behaviour such as region, age, sex, race, religion, policies of the parties, economic self-interest, media, party leaders, etc.

UNIT 2 - ELECTIONS, PARTIES AND POLICIES

Worksheet 2 - Twenty Questions: Students only tick a box if they agree with the statement. They obtain a plus or minus score for each tick. A tick for No.1 is -1; No.2 is +1; No.3 is +1; No.4 is +1; No.5 is -1; No.6 is -1; No.7 is +1; No.8 is +2; No.9 is +1; No.10 is -1; No.11 is +1; No.12 is -2; No.13 is -1; No.14 is +1; No.15 is -1; No.16 is -1; No.17 is -1; No.18 is -1; No.19 is +1; No.20 is +1. For example, if a student agreed with and ticked statements 5, 9, 12, 16 and 18 he would score -1,+1,-2,-1,-1 a total score of -4. The scores can then be plotted on the scale below.

Left	-4	0		Right
-11				+11

The maximum left-wing score is -11, the maximum right wing score is +11.

UNIT 3 - PARLIAMENT AND GOVERNMENT

The Government - Find Out:

1   The major difference is that the Government runs the country, Parliament scrutinises it, i.e. acts as a watchdog. Parliament also passes laws (most of which are proposed by the Government and pushed through using the Whip system). Power, therefore, resides with the Government - Parliament's role is secondary.

Hodder & Stoughton

© 1994 Paul Higginson. The publishers grant permission for multiple copies of this sheet to be made in the place of purchase for use solely in that institution.

3 Select Committees (groups of MPs who scrutinize the work of a particular government department), Question Time, letters to and meetings with Ministers, Standing Committees (act as a watchdog on Bills going through Parliament), House of Lords (has the power to amend and delay), vote of no-confidence (the ultimate sanction to bring down a government - rarely used) and Opposition Debates.

Worksheet 1 - The House of Commons:

Answers requiring specific knowledge.

1 Chairs debates, selects MPs to speak, keeps order, ensures a fair allocation of time between the parties, rules on points of order and procedure.

2 Front benches - Government on left, Opposition on right.

3 On right, in section furthest from Speaker's chair.

4 Historical device to prevent fights - lines are two sword lengths apart. MPs cannot cross them.

5 Honourable Gentlemen, Honourable Friend, Right Honourable (if they are members of the Privy Council, i.e. past or present Cabinet Ministers or party leaders). Aims to depersonalise debate and helps to retain a certain politeness and respect for opponents.

7 Could be to embarrass, to flatter, to criticise, to raise or score a point, to publicise oneself, to gain attention, to ingratiate oneself with the leader.

8 Prince Minister does not know what they will be.

14 Advantages are mainly concerned with providing the public with more information/knowledge. Disadvantages include TV trivialising politics, stressing personalities and hairstyles, rather than policies and important, but often unexciting, discussion. TV wants 'sound-bites' not lengthy complex debate.

Worksheet 3 - Freelandia - Crisis in Cabinet: As Cabinet Secretary, give out the photocopied news clips at appropriate moments during the simulation, usually when discussion dries up. Use the first 5 'clips' if Cabinet is 'hawk-ish', the last 5 'clips' if 'dove-ish'. Allow enough time at the end for the drafting of the press release.

UNIT 4 - PUBLIC SPENDING

Activities 2: A progressive tax like income tax means that the larger a taxpayer's income, the greater the proportion which is paid in tax. A regressive tax (such as VAT) is the reverse, i.e. the larger a taxpayer's income, the smaller the proportion paid in tax. A direct tax is applied to a person's income, an indirect tax to products and services.

Worksheet 2 - The Local Council: Follow-up work could be the writing of a press release outlining the reasons behind the cuts. After the simulation is over focus student attention on: a) the criteria used to decide on the cuts; b) the consequences of the cuts in terms of lost jobs, quality of services provided, public, media and pressure group reaction; c) the ways in which the councillors could defend their actions to the electorate when they next stand for re-election.

Worksheet 3 - Local Taxation:
1 Advantages include easy to understand and firm link to ability to pay. Disadvantages include large numbers who feel they are in too high a band (costly appeals system), does not overcome problem of local government lacking accountability.

4 Some on Conservative Right want education, police and fire services taken out of local government control, for example schools could receive an annual grant from central not local government (like new incorporated Further Education Sixth Form Colleges). Would significantly reduce power and status of local government, which might simply become an arm of central government.

Hodder & Stoughton   © 1994 Paul Higginson. The publishers grant permission for multiple copies of this sheet to be made in the place of purchase for use solely in that institution.

5 Pros - best way of ensuring taxation is linked to ability to pay. Cons - complex, might create a cycle of deprivation in inner cities (those in well paid jobs driven out, thereby increasing burden on those that remain), great regional variations from 4p in the £ (parts of Scotland) to 14.5p (Greenwich).

UNIT 5 - PRESSURE GROUPS

Activities 1: The AA (Automobile Association) is both a sectional group (it assists members who break down) and a cause group (it puts up road signs, campaigns for road safety, etc. for all road users).

Activities 2: Mention the undermining of unions by the Employment Acts of 1980, 1982 and 1984 which restricted 'closed shops', outlawed secondary picketing, took away legal immunities for unions on strike, introduced ballots before strike action and restricted official pickets to six. Discuss Mrs Thatcher's view that 'government should govern' and should not be swayed by the 'selfish' pressures of unions (or any pressure group). Also analyse 1979 'Winter of Discontent' and the view that unions were 'running the country'.

Worksheet 2 - Terminology: This exercise is best done as homework with students getting definitions from family and friends (who might be union members) and bringing the results back to class.)

Worksheet 3 - Strike!: As the Personnel Officer the teacher acts as intermediary between the two sides. The teacher should ensure (by giving out 'newsflashes' - make your own up or use the ones provided) that the workers vote for strike action. Note that under current legislation a strike-call must have the support of the majority of workers if it is to be implemented. Once the strike is underway bring the two sides together and attempt to negotiate a settlement. Debrief students after the simulation. Examine motives of both sides, the role of management and unions, and discuss whether the strike achieved anything. Address the issue of who has the most power in the dispute. Compare with the 1993 dispute at the Timex plant in Scotland - workers sacked, new ones employed, plant picketed. Timex closed down factory and relocated elsewhere. Compare the industrial disputes of the 1990s with those of the 1970s - how much power do trade unions have in Britain today?

UNIT 6 - THE LAW

Activity: The following cases relate to the criminal law: murder, graffiti, abusive language, shoplifting, train fare, racial discrimination, drunk and disorderly, speeding.

System of Courts:

1 Statistics show that they stand a better chance of winning their case before a jury than before a magistrate.

2 Contrast cheap, efficient, speedy system of decisions for minor cases, against unrepresentative of general population, out of touch, untrained, (a professional lawyer is more objective?), wide variations in sentencing across country.

Who are the Judges?

2 Examine ideas for making judiciary more representative (more ethnic minorities, women, younger people) reducing the historical trappings (gowns and wigs), televising court cases to make judiciary more accessible (as in Scotland), introducing a retirement age (65).

3 In some states of the US, judges are politically accountable i.e. they can be voted out of office if the public disapproves of their actions. Examine political accountability versus the need for political independence (the law is impartial/objective and should not be a hostage to popular political opinion).

Worksheet 1 - The Law and You: Answers: 1=18; 2=16; 3=16; 4=5; 5=14; 6=21; 7=18; 8=0; 9=18; 10=13; 11=18; 12=14; 13=16; 14=17; 15=16; 16=17; 17=16; 18=14; 19=21; and 20=10.

Hodder & Stoughton   © 1994 Paul Higginson. The publishers grant permission for multiple copies of this sheet to be made in the place of purchase for use solely in that institution.

Worksheet 2 - Legal Terminology: Solicitor=6; Legal Aid=1; Bail=9; Barrister=3; Law Lords=20; Magistrate=8; Indictable Offence=11; Summons=18; Community Service=5; Coroner=2; Stipendiary Magistrate=12; Summary Offence=19; Remand in custody=16; Judicial Review=14; Juvenile Court=17; Sue=4; Small claims court=15; Jury=7; Crown Prosecution Service=10; and Clerk of the Court=13.

Worksheet 3 - Trial by Jury: The teacher (especially if playing the Judge) must ensure that all sides stick to the facts outlined in the framework. Although a certain amount of extra detail and embellishment is acceptable and necessary the Judge must 'strike from the record' any remarks or suggestions by witnesses which are too extreme, for example, 'I saw Mr. Brent do it' - there were no witnesses to the crime. In the debriefing after the simulation examine how the jury reached its decision and analyse the effectiveness of this type of court system. Discussion could extend to recent miscarriages of justice such as the Birmingham Six.

UNIT 7 - EUROPE
Worksheet 1 - Map Work:

1 EC member states: Germany, France, Italy, Belgium, Holland, Luxembourg, UK, Ireland, Denmark, Greece, Spain and Portugal. EFTA states: Iceland, Norway, Sweden, Finland, Switzerland and Austria.

2 Estonia, Latvia, Lithuania, Poland, the Czech Republic, Slovakia, Hungary, States of the former Yugoslavia, Albania, Russia, Ukraine, Romania, Bulgaria, Turkey.

3 Euro-elections on June 9th 1994: a total of 567 MEPs elected. Germany (population 80m), Italy (58m), UK (57m) and France (56m) have 87 MEPs; Spain (39m) has 64; Netherlands (15m) has 31; Portugal, Greece, Belgium (all 10m each) have 25; Denmark (5m) has 16; Ireland (3.5m) has 15 and Luxembourg (0.4m) has 6.

Worksheet 2 - History: The correct historical dates for the events (in the order they are presented) are: 1981; 1957; 1986; 1945; 1975; 1959; 1956; 1973; 1991; 1992; 1986; 1990.

UNIT 8 - THE MEDIA
Worksheet 1 - The British Press:

1 Political affiliation column. All Conservative except: a) Mirror, Sunday Mirror, Sunday People, Financial Times, (all Labour though F.T. later back-tracked considerably; b) Observer, Guardian, Independent, and Independent on Sunday lean towards the centre, Labour Right.

5 People cutting back in time of recession, relying more on TV and radio for news, etc. However, stories on topics such as the Royal marriages and the election in 1992 helped to boost sales dramatically at specific times of the year.

Worksheet 3 - The TV News: Emphasise to students that only between five and eight stories can be effectively covered in a four minute bulletin, so before they write their script they should select the items they wish to include. Groups should not be allowed more than eight items. Suggest that perhaps one member from each team writes a 45 second script for each item. Allow groups only one practice run (to simulate the immediacy and tension of a real bulletin) and place strict time limits and deadlines on each phase of the exercise. If you want to make the simulation even more real, throw in another major newsflash two minutes before transmission time. If you have a video camera this is a useful exercise to film and replay later.

UNIT 9 - POVERTY
Groups Affected by Poverty - Questions:

3 Hairdressing, shop work, cleaning, textiles, catering, some office work. Many of these workers are part-time or temporary (and most are not unionised) and therefore not well paid. Many are married women.

© 1994 Paul Higginson. The publishers grant permission for multiple copies of this sheet to be made in the place of purchase for use solely in that institution.

4 Governments of all parties have increased the purchasing power of the state pension (partly for electoral reasons - there are 9 million pensioner voters!). Also growth in number of private pension plans and increase in house prices for owner occupiers.

Rich and Poor - Questions:

3 Examine arguments for re-distribution (fairness, justice, creating communities, helping less well-off, etc.) and against (focus on the creation of a 'dependency culture', permanent 'underclass', saps initiative etc.). What effect does poverty have on the crime rate? Does re-distribution cut crime?

4 Examine lifestyle as well as income.

UNIT 10 - GENDER

Women in Politics - Questions:

1 Socialisation process, sexism from party selection committees, idea that voters prefer male candidates, not an interesting career for women (long hours, low pay), hours in the Commons are not conducive to family life, and so on.

2 Men were better candidates, sexist voters, women usually selected for 'difficult to win seats'. The latter is the actual reason.

3 Examine the pros and cons of positive discrimination. Pros include: just, proportional, only way to break down centuries of sexism. Cons include: unfair to men, women should achieve on merit alone, etc.

4 Change hours of sitting of Parliament (e.g. abolish all-night sitting), PM could be forced to include more women in his Cabinet to act as role-models, non-sexist political education in schools, programmes to encourage women to get involved in politics at all levels (trade unions, local government, pressure groups, etc.), create a Ministry for Women.

5 Can your class name any female contemporary British political/public figures apart from Mrs Thatcher and the Royal Family? Any Cabinet Ministers, industrialists, trade union leaders, police officers, judges, university professors, diplomats, leaders of other countries?

Equality and the Law - Questions:

1 Men get more promotions, do more full time work, get the better jobs, etc.

2 Examine the criteria used to decide equal value. If hard work were the measuring stick then would nurses earn the same as TV presenters?

What Happened When?: The correct order of dates for the events is 1928, 1919, 1992, 1969, 1905, 1979, 1919, 1958.

Worksheet 2 - Woman and Work: The correct answers are: 1c; 2a; 3c; 4c; 5b; 6c; 7c; 8a; 9c; 10b; 11b and 12c.

Worksheet 3 - The Ordination of Women: Brief counter-arguments might be:
1 Priests do not impersonate Jesus (or they would all have long hair and beards!) - they bring God to people, and God has no sex.
2 There were cultural reasons for this: at that time it would have been very difficult for Jesus to have included women in the group that travelled with him.
3 Jesus makes no mention of other important contemporary issues like contraception or inter-faith marriages.
4 It has to start sometime.
5 Respected yes, but the majority view must prevail.
6 Can't be helped, given time the Catholic Church may also come round to the idea.
7 Nonsense - Mrs Thatcher!
8 This is just an excuse for discrimination. Women's roles mean church cleaning and flower arranging.

Hodder & Stoughton

© 1994 Paul Higginson. The publishers grant permission for multiple copies of this sheet to be made in the place of purchase for use solely in that institution.

9 Male priests have children too!

10 Progressive change would never occur if this view prevailed.

11 Priest represents Christ, does not impersonate him.

12 Can't be helped. If it's right it must be good for the Church in the long run.

UNIT 11 - RACE AND ETHNIC MINORITIES

Worksheet 3 - Racial Discrimination True or False:

1 True (T). Between 1962 and 82 there was a total outflow of 700,000.

2 False (F). It is 5.5%.

3 False. Niranjan Dera became the first Asian Tory MP in 1992.

4 True

5 False. The National Front was reported to have had this number in the 1970s. Membership is now probably in the hundreds rather than thousands.

6 True. On the grounds that all members of the party must promote anti-racism, not just one section.

7 True. Compared to 22% for whites. Figures for women are 1% Afro-Caribbean, 9% white.

8 False. Bill Morris - TGWU.

9 False. It will increase by 0.5% to 6%.

10 False. Only 31% (79% for whites).

11 False. It was 35%.

12 True.

13 True. Britain has always had a mixed culture including Celts, Romans, Danes, Normans, Saxons, Irish, New Commonwealth.

14 False. It is - under the Race Relations Act and EC law.

15 True. 74% of Asians, 64% of whites own their own home.

16 True. 1,500.

17 False. Haringey has the highest with 30% (Leicester has 22%).

18 True.

19 False. It is 35%.

20 False. They are twice as likely to enter higher education.

UNIT 12 - CRIME AND PUNISHMENT

Levels of Crime - Questions:

3 Affluence has led to more cars, there is more off-street parking, it has become a lucrative 'business' for some professional car thieves, etc.

4 Example - burglary rate in inner cities/deprived areas is 1 in 10 houses per annum. In rural/better off/retirement areas it is 1 in 1,000. Most crime is committed in the locality where the offender lives.

5 People don't bother to report crime. They may: a) think it is not serious enough; b) know it won't be solved; c) feel they would be wasting police time; d) be afraid (as in rape); e) have no

Hodder & Stoughton

© 1994 Paul Higginson. The publishers grant permission for multiple copies of this sheet to be made in the place of purchase for use solely in that institution.

confidence in police; f) be unwilling to report it (e.g. domestic violence). Also, not enough police to effectively record the crime that does occur?

6   More rapes committed; police paying more attention to this crime and handling cases in a more sensitive manner; courts and Press more sympathetic to victims; public more aware of the crime and less willing to let offenders get away with it.

7   Telephones make it much easier to report crimes. Insurance companies require burglaries, car theft, etc. to be reported to police before they pay compensation.

Worksheet 1 - Crime Quiz: Answers 1c; 2a; 3c; 4b; 5c; 6c; 7a; 8b; 9a; 10c; 11c; 12a and 13a.

Worksheet 2 - You are the Magistrate: A real magistrate working in Outer London examined these cases and came up with the following sentences (note that other JPs in other parts of the country may well make different conclusions, i.e. there are no 'answers' to this exercise).

Speeding - A=£250; B=£40; C=£50; D=£200 and no disqualification because of 'exceptional hardship'.

Shoplifting - F=Probation order (2 years) or possibly a short period of imprisonment (this would depend on the psychiatric reports). G=Conditional discharge or £50 fine. H=Fine (this would be based on social enquiry reports - probably £100). J=£200 fine.

Pub fight - X=3 months imprisonment. Y=Community Service plus £150 compensation order to victim. Z=Community Service or small fine. N.B. Drunkenness is rarely, if ever, seen as a mitigating factor. (In order to help magistrates in such cases there are guidelines which distinguish between a 'more' or 'less' serious offence. More serious: extensive injuries; deliberate kicking; group action; pre-meditated action; victim particularly vulnerable; use of weapon. Less serious: minor injury; impulsive; provocation. Get students to decide, before they sentence, whether offences are 'more' or 'less' serious.)

Hodder & Stoughton © 1994 Paul Higginson. The publishers grant permission for multiple copies of this sheet to be made in the place of purchase for use solely in that institution.

1 What is Politics?

'Labour and Tories neck and neck in opinion polls.'
'Fears grow over Islamic nuclear bomb.'
'Greenpeace launches campaign against nuclear energy.'
"Clean our filthy streets," says local councillor.
'Home Secretary under pressure as crime rate soars.'
'IRA bomb explodes in London.'
'"Students over 16 years of age should get grants to stay on at school," says backbench MP.'

DEFINITIONS

How can politics be defined? Here are some views on what politics is all about.

'Politics is about persuading people to do things you want them to do.'
'It's about running a country - we cannot all be in charge, so we have a government to run things on our behalf.'
'Politics is a way a nation or group manages conflicts and disagreements without the use of force. If violence is used to solve a problem, politics will have failed.'
'It's an academic discipline studied by political scientists, students and journalists.'
'Office politics is about stabbing people in the back and keeping in with the boss.'
'Politics is all about trying to find the best system of government - it's based on ideals like Democracy and Communism. It's about making the world a better place in which to live.'
'Politics has got nothing to do with me.'
'As society evolves we must find ways of coping with change - increased technology leads to high unemployment. That's a political problem which requires a political solution.'
Politics is about power.'
'Everything and everyone has a political dimension. We are all political animals and everything in existence can be seen in a political light.'

❏ Questions

1 Which of these views do you agree with and why?

2 Which view comes closest to your own view of politics?

3 'Politics is about everything.' Is this true? Make a list of objects in the room or things you can see, and try to find a connection with politics, for example: Teacher - should his/her pay be increased by the government? Pen - should cheap imports be allowed in from overseas to damage British industry? Textbooks - should students buy their own, or should the government provide money for free textbooks for all? Air - should we be looking to clean up our air by electing a party committed to improving the environment?

Try to find something which has no connection whatsoever with Politics!

PROBLEM SOLVING

Politics is essentially about problem solving. The following extract examines a conflict situation which politicians have to try and resolve.

Britain's involvement in Northern Ireland began in the twelfth century, but the modern conflict stems from the sixteenth and seventeenth centuries. During the Reformation most of Britain converted to Protestantism, while Ireland remained Roman Catholic. In order to keep political control of Ireland the British Government encouraged Protestants to settle in Ireland, especially in the northern six counties (Ulster). A Protestant land-owning elite was established and Catholics suffered great discrimination. In 1920 - 1921 Northern Ireland was separated from the rest of Ireland (Partition), and in 1948 the predominantly Catholic South became an independent state ¨ the Republic. Tension in the North continued however (62 per cent of the population being Protestant, 38 per cent Catholic). Most

© 1994 Paul Higginson. The publishers grant permission for multiple copies of this sheet to be made in the place of purchase for use solely in that institution.

Hodder & Stoughton

Protestants are Unionists opposed to a united Ireland, determined to keep links (union) with Britain. Most Catholics are Nationalists, and blame Britain for a false division of their country - they see a united Ireland as the best solution. Although various paramilitary groups had existed for some time, it was during the 1960s that the IRA (Irish Republican Army) and the UVF (Ulster Volunteer Force) dramatically intensified the use of violence and terror to try and achieve their objectives. As law and order began to break down the British Government sent troops in, and imposed direct rule from London.

Questions and discussion

1 Identify and evaluate three possible political solutions to the conflict in Ireland.

2 What are the pros and cons of using force to achieve an objective?

3 'In a democracy the majority view must prevail.' What relevance has this quote to the Irish situation?

DEMOCRACY

Democracy is a key concept in politics. The term comes from two Greek words and literally means 'power to the people'. In the fifth century BC in Athens, citizens were expected to take part in the running of the city. Public debate, elections and majority voting were common - this was a form of direct democracy with citizens actively participating in decision making. In twentieth-century Britain it is impossible for us all to gather in the city square to voice our opinions, so we elect representatives who run the country on our behalf.

❑ Questions

1 'British democracy consists of putting a cross in a box every five years when we hand over power to someone else.' Is this true?

2 In Australia you are fined if you don't vote in elections. Why is this? Do you think people should be compelled to participate?

3 Democracy can be interpreted as participation in the decision making process and taking more control over our own lives. In what ways, other than voting, can we get personally involved in politics?

4 'If voting changed anything, they'd abolish it.' (Ken Livingstone) What does this comment mean, and do you agree with it?

❖ Discussion Point - The Death Penalty

In a democracy the wishes of the majority prevail, but is the majority always right, or morally superior? Recent opinion polls suggest that a large majority of the British people is in favour of bringing back hanging for serious crimes. Our elected representatives in Parliament, however, have consistently opposed the re-introduction of the death penalty (also by a large majority). Should this happen in a democracy? Should our elected politicians lead, or merely try to reflect public opinion?

CONSTITUTION

A constitution consists of the rules and practices by which a country is governed. It is usually written in one document (although Britain's constitution is said to be unwritten as it cannot be found in one single document). Below are examples of rules which can be found in the US constitution:

- Presidents must be at least 35 years old.
- Citizens have freedom of speech, worship and peaceful assembly.
- The people have a right to bear arms (carry guns).
- If the President dies or resigns, the Vice President takes over.

Rules are essential in government if people's rights are to be protected and dictatorship or tyranny prevented.

Hodder & Stoughton   *© 1994 Paul Higginson. The publishers grant permission for multiple copies of this sheet to be made in the place of purchase for use solely in that institution.*

Problem Solving

Politics is about problem solving. Listed below are ten current problems that politicians are expected to solve. If you were involved in politics how would you try to deal with these problems?

Choose **five** problems and write possible solutions in the boxes below; then discuss your ideas with the group.

High youth unemployment	
Rise in levels of violent crime	
Shortage of teachers in schools	
Spread of AIDS	
Homelessness/people sleeping rough on the streets	
Spread of under-age drinking	
Increased pollution	
Over-crowding in prisons	
Traffic congestion	
Famine in Africa	

Hodder & Stoughton

© 1994 Paul Higginson. *The publishers grant permission for multiple copies of this sheet to be made in the place of purchase for use solely in that institution.*

Writing a Constitution

Imagine you have to write a new constitution. This could be for a new country (e.g. the recent new states in the former USSR or Yugoslavia), or simply a new school or college club/society (e.g. Film Club, Politics Society).

Decide the rules by which the country or society should be governed.

Elect or choose someone to act as secretary then write your constitution.

Areas to cover include:

a) Do you have one leader, or a committee, or no leader at all? If you want a president or chairperson, how are you going to elect him or her?

b) What functions and powers does the leader/committee have? How long will they remain in office?

c) How will decisions be made?

d) What happens to those who break the rules?

e) What happens if a minority disagrees with the policies the group is following? What if it wants to break away and become independent?

f) How often will the whole group meet to discuss policy?

g) How will you guard against tyranny, i.e. one person or group taking overall control?

If you are drawing up a constitution for a new nation, there are many other points to consider including:

a) What rights do you want to safeguard ¨ free speech, freedom of religion, right to remain silent, right to a job, right to own your own house, right to a certain minimum level of income, rights of the unborn, right to carry guns?

b) At what age should people be able to vote. Should voting be compulsory? Do you want to state a minimum age for office holders (e.g. President)?

c) Will the death penalty be an acceptable (i.e. constitutional) form of punishment?

Hodder & Stoughton

© *1994 Paul Higginson. The publishers grant permission for multiple copies of this sheet to be made in the place of purchase for use solely in that institution.*

Many politicians, including John Major, have wanted to create a classless society; but throughout history in all countries there has been social stratification, a division of society into different groupings. In Britain today it is estimated that almost one-half of the population can be described as middle class, just over one-half as working class. But how do you determine a person's class? Do you think that you belong to a particular social class?

Answer the questions below.

1 Occupation of father/mother

2 Type of school attended

3 Career plan

4 Area in which you live

5 Hobbies and interests

6 Favourite sport

7 Political party you support

8 Political party your parents support

9 Newspaper you read

10 Favourite drink

11 What social class do you think you belong to?

The above questions are designed simply to stimulate discussion - there are no hard and fast rules which determine class. **Some people say that class no longer exists. What is your view?**

The British Market Research Society uses occupation as the most important factor in defining class. Society is divided into five classes, one of which is further sub-divided:

Middle Class
    A   Professional - Doctor, Lawyer
    B   Managerial - Manager, Teacher
    C1   Clerical - Police, Bank Clerk
Working Class
    C2   Skilled manual - Plumber, Electrician
    D   Unskilled or manual - Roadsweeper, General labourer
    E   Residual - OAP, widow

The BMRS, and political scientists, no longer use the classification 'upper class' as it is such a tiny fraction of the population. The aristocracy is now classified as middle class.

✪ Further study

1 'You are whatever class you think you are.' Do you agree?

2 How far does class influence the way you vote?

3 How easy is it to move from one class to another?

4 Are class divisions in Britain breaking down or getting stronger?

Hodder & Stoughton

© 1994 Paul Higginson. The publishers grant permission for multiple copies of this sheet to be made in the place of purchase for use solely in that institution.

2 Elections, Parties and Policies

ELECTIONS

The Prime Minister decides when a general election is to be fought. Although elections must be held at least once very five years, the Prime Minister may call an election at any time - perhaps if his party is well ahead in the opinion polls. For the general election, the country is divided up into 651 constituencies or areas, each with roughly the same number of voters. Each constituency elects one Member of Parliament (MP), and the party with the majority of MPs wins the election.

VOTING SYSTEMS

Britain's voting system is called 'first past the post' as the candidate with the most votes in each constituency is elected as an MP, even though he may have less than 50 per cent of the votes cast. So if Jane Smith gets 35 per cent of the votes, Ted Jones 33 per cent and Sue Carter 32 per cent, Jane wins, even though 65 per cent of the voters prefer someone else. Taken over the whole country this can mean that a party can win the election without having the support of the majority of the voters.

So in the 1992 election the Conservatives gained more that half the seats, even though they achieved only 43 per cent of the votes.

The Liberal Democrats and some politicians from other parties are in favour of a different voting system called 'proportional representation' (PR; used in all Western European countries except

PARTY	SEATS	% VOTE
Conservative	336	43
Labour	273	35
Liberal Democrats	20	18
Others	24	4

France). There are many types of PR but the one preferred by the Liberal Democrats is the Single Transferable Vote (STV) system. Under this system the number of constituencies would be reduced to 143 and instead of voting with a single cross, voters would number the candidates in order of preference.

The main arguments for PR are:

1   It is proportional, so if a party gained 50 per cent of the vote it would receive approximately 50 per cent of the seats in the Commons, if it gained 20 per cent of the vote it would get 20 per cent of the seats and so on.

2   Coalitions of two or more parties would be formed and these would be more representative of public opinion because they would represent at least 50 per cent of the voters.

3   It would encourage parties to work together rather than to continually oppose each other, leading to continuity of policy.

The main arguments for retaining the first past the post system are:

1   It allows a voter to choose a constituency MP, who is the single representative for a reasonably small area.

2   Coalitions lead to weak, indecisive and unstable government - some countries with PR have frequent elections when coalitions break up.

3   Small parties often hold the balance of power in a hung Parliament and they can then 'blackmail' the other parties. This can lead to backroom deals between parties on policies after the election.

Hodder & Stoughton

© 1994 Paul Higginson. The publishers grant permission for multiple copies of this sheet to be made in the place of purchase for use solely in that institution.

1   Find out the name of your constituency, your local MP and the party he/she represents.

2   If PR had existed in 1992, how many seats would each party have gained?

3   Which party or parties would have formed the government?

4   Do coalitions produce good or bad government?

POLITICAL PARTIES

When you are 18 you can vote in an election for one of the political parties. The two largest are the Conservative and Labour parties, but there are smaller parties including the Liberal Democrats, Greens, Scottish Nationalist Party, National Front, Plaid Cymru, Ulster Unionists and Social Democratic and Labour Party (SDLP).

The main principles of the three largest parties are outlined below.

THE CONSERVATIVE PARTY

'We believe in a free enterprise economy with very little state interference. Personal freedom, individuality, choice, incentive and opportunity are the bases of our philosophy. By creating a thriving market economy, we can create wealth and thereby support improvements in social services, maintain law and order and provide for the defence of our country'.

THE LABOUR PARTY

'Our aim is to achieve a more just, equal and democratic society. The state should play an active role in helping the underdogs in society, and in developing effective public services like the NHS and education. Some key industries should be publicly owned and the wealth produced by all should be fairly shared by all. Tax cuts should not be made (especially for high earners) if they mean a decline in public services'.

THE LIBERAL DEMOCRATS

'Unlike the parties of the left and right we speak for the nation as a whole rather than one specific group or class. We believe in the protection of civil liberties, social justice, decentralised government and a new electoral system (proportional representation). We support a mixed economy involving public and private enterprise and place great stress on Europe, conservation of the environment, and education'.

■ Activity

In groups of three make sure you understand all the principles outlined above. Underline the ideas you support, and discuss them in your group, then feed back to the whole class.

Each party has basic principles or general aims, but it also has specific and detailed ideas on how the country should be run. On each subject area or issue a party will develop specific policies, for example taxation is an important issue today. Conservative policy states that we can decrease the tax we pay while maintaining good public services. Labour policy states that in order to achieve effective public services tax should not be reduced (indeed high earners should pay more).

■ Activity

Which of the following issues do you consider to be the most important in Britain today? Foreign and defence policy (including nuclear weapons); Economy; Employment; Environment; Trade unions; Health and social security; Housing; Law and order; Local government (includes local tax); Education; Equal opportunities; Overseas aid; Transport; Europe.

1   Place them in order of importance, 1 to 14. Work on your own.

2   Working in groups of three, compare your answers and produce a joint list for the whole group (arrive at a group consensus through discussion).

3   Compare your list with those of other groups in the class.

Hodder & Stoughton   *© 1994 Paul Higginson. The publishers grant permission for multiple copies of this sheet to be made in the place of purchase for use solely in that institution.*

General Election Policies 1992

The Issues	Conservative	Labour	Lib Dem
Taxation	Continue tax cuts, ambition of 20% basic rate; inheritance tax only for very rich, 40% rate on estate over £500,000; seek one tax-free account for every saver; council tax, revalue homes every three years	Top rate 50%, earnings threshold "well over" £30,000; reverse last week's budget changes; abolish ceiling on 9% national insurance contributions; new tax on unearned income (pensioners exempt)	Add 1p to basic rate if necessary; increase tax threshold; abolish mortgage relief for new borrowers, replace with "housing cost relief"
Industry	Privatise British Coal, BR; require trade unionists to opt in annually to unions; individuals to sue unlawful strikers in public sector; protection for works on personal contracts through industrial tribunal	National economic assessment, dual budget-public spending announcement; National Investment Bank, private capital for public projects; tax incentives for investors	Combine Monopolies and Mergers Commission with OFT, power to break up privatised monopolies; BT break-up; more private rail services; new restrictive practices act
Health	Extend opt-out hospitals, fund-holding GPs; increase spending, extra £2.7 billion next year; two-year maximum waiting time for patients; performance league tables; private treatment if NHS inadequate	End GP fund-holding, opt-out hospitals to health authorities; Department of Health and Community Care (renamed); right to smoke-free environment at work; free eye tests, dental checks	End GP fund-holding, NHS trusts; more freedom for doctors to refer patients to chosen hospitals; free eye tests, dental checks; salaried GPs, accredited specialists
Education	Extend city technology colleges, grant-maintained schools, opt-outs; performance-related teachers' pay; teachers, governors to control 80% school budgets by 1994; retain A-level gold standard	Abolish city technology colleges, grant-maintained schools back to council control; review private schools' charitable status, phase out assisted places scheme; reform A-levels	Return city technology colleges, grand-maintained schools to council control; review private schools' charitable status, phase out assisted places scheme; reform A-levels
Training	Tax relief possible for companies improving training schemes	Skills UK, new organisation to direct training policy; employers to pay 0.5% of payroll on training; right for 16-year-olds to stay at school or traineeship based on National Training Qualifications	Require working 16 to 19-year-olds to undergo education, training two days a week; return further education colleges to local authorities; adult education fees for fixed period to key groups
Defence	Order fourth Trident, 512 warheads; 6% defence budget over four years; "options for change" review, cut 116,000 soldiers; retain autonomy, subservient to neither Nato nor European Community	Cancel fourth Trident order depending on contractual position and cost; "no first-use" policy for nuclear weapons, end British nuclear testing; Defence Diversification Agency	Limit warheads on four Trident submarines to same (192) or fewer than Polaris; cut £1 billion (50%) from military research, savings to civil research; "significant reduction" in armaments
Law and order	Reorganise police service, nominate police chief for every town; identify potential criminals among children as young as six; monitor police response, satisfaction with service.	Increase police numbers over lifetime of parliament; body to investigate miscarriages of justice; Sentencing Council for consistency in punishment orders prisoners' ombudsman	Extend Court of Appeal powers; regional appeal courts; Judicial Services Commission to nominate judges; public defender to investigate miscarriages of justice; plea-bargaining
Environment	Environment Protection Agency; develop wind, wave, solar power; stabilise carbon dioxide emissions by 2005; phase out CFC emissions by 2000; "green" taxes; extra green-belt protection	Appoint "green minister", Environmental Protection Executive; stabilise then cut carbon dioxide emissions by year 2000; cut Vat on environment-friendly goods; return water companies to public sector	Energy taxes to cut industrial gases; "pollution-added tax" on damaging goods; cut carbon dioxide emissions 30% by 2005, sulphur dioxide by 60% in five years; Environmental Protection Agency
Social policy	Increase pensions, child benefit annually in line with inflation; improve disablement benefits; unemployment, sickness, income support benefits in line with inflation; cut benefit delays	Pensions up £5 a week (single), £8 (couple), linked to average earnings or prices; flexible retirement age; child benefit up to £9.95; minister for children, children's rights commissioner	Priority increases in pensions, £5 (single), £8 (couple); increase child benefit by £1 a week per child

Hodder & Stoughton

© 1994 Paul Higginson. The publishers grant permission for multiple copies of this sheet to be made in the place of purchase for use solely in that institution.

Employment	Extend performance-related public-sector pay; assist people to join union of their choice, union leaders to disclose salaries, stop abuse of "check off" of union dues.	Minimum wage, at least half average male earnings (£3.40 an hour), £10,000 fine and three months' prison for offending employers; Industrial Court; statutory duty to promote equal treatment	Cut jobless by 400,000 in year; job-creation/training programme costing £3 billion; jobless to improve council homes, other buildings; secondment of redundant executives to small businesses
Local government	Replace two-tier system, more unitary local authorities; cabinet-style councils; performance tables for councils; retain uniform business rate	Regional tier in England, elected regional government in second term; strategic authority for London elected by PR; Quality Commission, "customer contracts" for residents, annual satisfaction surveys	Ombudsman for every council; compensation for sub-standard services; public question times at council meetings, "neighbourhood committees"; uniform business rate replaced by site-value rating
Housing	Boost home ownership to 75%; rent-into-mortgage scheme for council tenants; mortgage-rescue schemes, stamp duty relief until August; possibly subsidies for conversions, e.g. flats above shops	National Housing Bank; phased release council house sale receipts; leaseholders' right to buy freeholds collectively or extend leases; outlaw "gazumping"	Mortgage-to-rent scheme; building societies take ownership, seek rent to get 8% return on capital; support shared ownership; reform housing benefit system, pay claimants in advance of need, lend deposits
Transport	Continue £12 billion road building, double trunk road programme over 10 years; BR privatisation white paper; compensation for delayed travellers	Halt BR privatisation moves; transport safety inspectorate; strengthen passenger watchdogs; halt road schemes not yet out to contract; "traffic-calming" bus-priority schemes, cycle routes	Increase petrol prices substantially, fuel taxes linked to pollution emission; phase out vehicle excise duty, "road-pricing"; private rail lines, high-speed link Channel to north and west
Arts and media	Protect "listed" art works from export; extra finance for museum purchases; support "Millennium Fund" to repair national museums and construct new buildings; devolve Arts Council power.	Ministry for Arts and Media; phase out museum, art gallery charges; ownership of TV companies and newspapers to Monopolies and Mergers Commission; abolish Broadcasting Standards Council	Ministry for Arts and Communications, arts spending to 1% GDP; broadcasting act, renew BBC charter responsibilities, abolish Broadcasting Standards Council; lift Sinn Fein broadcasting ban
Constitution	Categorically opposed to proportional representation and devolution to Scotland, Wales or English regions; streamline Whitehall departments	Replace Lords with elected second chamber, proportional representation for Scottish assembly; freedom of information act; Commons committee on security services	PR; incorporate European Convention on Human Rights, move to bill of human rights, written constitution; Senate replaces Lords; home rule for Scotland, Wales; fixed-term parliaments
Equal opportunities	Opportunity 2000, encourage promotion of talented women and ethnic minorities, but against positive discrimination	Ministry for Women, cabinet minister; simplify, extend race equality laws; citizenship law to respect "family life"; strengthen laws on rape, domestic violence	Wide-ranging initiatives across all policy areas
Scotland	Oppose devolution or independence but ready to consider higher Westminster profile for Scottish interests; abolish regional authorities; privatise forestry commission and tourist board	Scottish parliament in Edinburgh in first year, legislative and revenue-raising powers, elected by "additional member" PR, limited power to vary tax, plus contribution from UK taxation	Home rule for Scotland; Scottish assembly logical consequence of European union; power over all policy except defence, foreign affairs and large-scale economics
Wales	Oppose devolution or independence but ready to consider higher Westminster profile for Welsh interests; redraw local government map, 23 new all-purpose authorities such as Pembrokeshire	Directly elected Welsh assembly, single-tier "most-purpose" local authorities; Welsh language act, fair treatment of daily users; Welsh-medium schooling for all families wanting it	Welsh language act; offer Welsh-medium schooling to all families who want it
Northern Ireland	Support Anglo-Irish agreement, continue to promote all-party talks suspended in pre-election period	Review prevention of terrorism act; end strip-searching, plastic bullets; support Anglo-Irish agreement; creation of united Ireland by consent	Support Anglo-Irish agreement, reject coalition with Unionists
Europe	Minister for European Affairs of cabinet rank; reject imposition of single currency or European Central Bank removing control of economic policy; retain control of immigration, drugs, anti-terrorist policy	Support single currency development if there is "real convergence" between British and EC economies; sign social charter immediately; develop European environment charter	Single European currency, independent central bank, move to narrow band of ERM soon as possible; political integration, Euro-citizenship; Rapid Response Force, peace-keeping, disaster relief

(© Sunday Times 15 March '92)

Hodder & Stoughton

© 1994 Paul Higginson. The publishers grant permission for multiple copies of this sheet to be made in the place of purchase for use solely in that institution.

Your Political Views

■ **Activity**

Analyse the policies put forward by the Labour and Conservative parties at the 1992 General Election, as they are set out on Worksheets 1 and 2. If you agree with the policy, put a tick next to it; put a cross next to those you disagree with.

Underline anything you are unsure about or don't fully understand and bring this up in class discussion.

TWENTY QUESTIONS

To find out whether you are Left-wing, Right-wing or in the centre study the following policy statements. If you are unsure of the meaning of a particular statement discuss it with your teacher and your group. Put a tick if you agree with the statement.

1 School students should receive a grant if they stay on at school after 16.　　———

2 Able-bodied people who refuse jobs they are offered should have their dole money stopped.　———

3 The government should cut down on crime by increasing prison sentences.　———

4 The death penalty should be re-introduced.　———

5 British troops should withdraw from Northern Ireland.　———

6 Tax should be raised in order to increase spending on the National Health Service.　———

7 Council house tenants should continue to be able to buy their own homes.　———

8 Immigrants should be sent back to their own countries.　———

9 Stricter laws should be introduced to regulate trade unions' power.　———

10 Laws should be introduced to prevent discrimination against homosexuals.　———

11 The government should spend as much money as is necessary to maintain a strong defence in the Falkland Isles.　———

12 Everyone should receive roughly the same salary whatever they do.　———

13 Britain should adopt proportional representation for general elections.　———

14 Private education (public schools) should be encouraged as an alternative to the state system.　———

15 Nuclear power stations should be phased out.　———

16 The Royal Family should be replaced with an elected president.　———

17 Scotland and Wales should have their own elected Assemblies.　———

18 Britain should give up its nuclear weapons whatever other countries decide.　———

19 Taxes should be cut and public spending reduced.　———

20 Most of the remaining public industries should be privatised.　———

Hodder & Stoughton

© 1994 Paul Higginson. The publishers grant permission for multiple copies of this sheet to be made in the place of purchase for use solely in that institution.

Form Your Own Political Party

Get into groups of four or five.

You are going to form a new political party which will contest the next general election. You need to do the following things:

1 Decide how you are going to choose the leader of the party. How are you going to elect him/her?

2 Elect the leader (who will then chair the meetings), and a secretary.

3 Decide on the following:

 a) Will the leader always have the final decision on policy matters? or

 b) Will you decide policies democratically (one man/woman, one vote)?

 c) A name for the party.

 d) An election slogan.

4 Produce a policy statement (one or two sentences) on each priority issue i.e. decide party aims. The priority issues are:

- NHS
- Schools/Education
- Foreign Affairs (including Europe)
- Local Government (including local tax)
- Defence (including nuclear weapons)

- Health & Social Services
- Law and Order
- Economy
- Environment

 You must now prioritise these issues i.e. put them in order of importance (from one to nine. Which policies do you want to stress most to the electorate?

5 Produce a five-minute party political broadcast to put forward the position of your party to the electorate. Decide:

 a) what you are going to say;

 b) who is going to say it;

 c) how you are going to say it. How will you use visual aids? Method of presentation, etc.

 If you have a video these broadcasts can be recorded and shown to the whole group or at assembly.

Hodder & Stoughton

© 1994 Paul Higginson. The publishers grant permission for multiple copies of this sheet to be made in the place of purchase for use solely in that institution.

3 Parliament & Government

The British Parliament consists of three parts:

1 The monarch or sovereign, now with very little real power.

2 The House of Lords (over 1,100 members, including 760 hereditary peers with inherited titles, 340 life peers, 26 bishops and archbishops, and nine Law Lords).

3 The House of Commons (651 elected MPs).

Although the House of Commons was once the weakest part of Parliament it is now the most powerful. The Commons takes the primary role in making laws, controlling the country's finances, and acting as a watchdog over government policies.

MAKING LAWS

Most laws are initiated by the government. Each parliamentary session begins with the Queen's Speech, a programme of proposed laws that the Prime Minister hopes to pass in the year ahead. On average around 100 new laws are made each year.

THE BACKBENCH MP

MPs who are not members of the government or Opposition front benches are backbenchers. They debate and vote in the Commons, take part in committee work, and keep in close contact with constituents and pressure groups. Here is an extract from the diary of a typical busy backbench MP.

9.00	Arrive at Commons and examine post - 20 letters from constituents, 15 circulars, leaflets from pressure groups, etc.
10.30	Standing Committee looking at a bill on education reform.
1.00	Lunch with representatives from Shelter (a pressure group helping the homeless).
2.00	Environment Question Time in Commons chamber.
3.15	Prime Minister's Question Time.
4.00	Meeting with other backbenchers to discuss party policy on defence.
5.30	More paperwork on correspondence, phone calls to constituency.
6.30	Dinner with constituents who oppose plans for the siting of a new nuclear power plant in the constituency.
7.30	Debate on the police in the House - make a speech, vote.
9.30	Brief interview with local newspaper reporter on nuclear issue.
10.30	Appear on BBC's Newsnight to discuss police debate.

❖ Discussion

1 Who or what should MPs be loyal to?
- their constituents
- the party
- their conscience
- the good of the country
- the pressure group they support

Consider the case of the above MP, who believes strongly that nuclear power is wrong and who is a member of Friends of the Earth (which opposes the plant). His party policy however is to support nuclear energy, and most of his constituents (and local trade unions) appear to want the power plant as it will create thousands of new jobs in an unemployment blackspot. What should the MP do?

Hodder & Stoughton   © 1994 Paul Higginson. The publishers grant permission for multiple copies of this sheet to be made in the place of purchase for use solely in that institution.

2 MPs earn about the same as a deputy head in a medium-sized school (they have an additional allowance for office costs like stationery, postage and secretarial work). This is about half the salary of their counterparts in Germany. Do you think they are over-paid or under-paid? Should they be paid by results? or by how much time they spend in the Commons?

THE HOUSE OF LORDS

The Lords' main functions are to check and if necessary amend legislation, debate important topics, and act as a general watchdog on government activities. The Law Lords also constitute the final appeal court in the land. Many feel the House of Lords should be abolished or reformed, while others want it to continue as it is.

"The Lords are an undemocratic, hereditary aristocratic elite. They do not represent the nation ¨women, ethnic minorities, the young, the working class, the political left are poorly represented. We should scrap the Lords and have an elected second chamber."

"The Lords play a vital role in Parliament. They relieve the Commons of a great deal of work, provide useful amendments to Bills, and are free of the party political pressures that hinder debate in the Commons. The House of Lords is the oldest second chamber in the world and the expertise and wisdom of peers has served the nation well over the years."

What is your view?

THE GOVERNMENT

After the general election the leader of the winning party becomes the Prime Minister (PM). He or she then selects about 20 Ministers to form the Cabinet, and about 80 Junior Ministers. The Prime Minister and the team of Ministers form the government; they are responsible for running the country on a day to day basis. Most Ministers are MPs who sit in the Commons, though some are chosen from the House of Lords. Each Cabinet minister is responsible for running a particular department, such as Defence or Environment, and he or she is advised and assisted by a team of civil servants.

✪ Further study

Find out:

1 the major difference between Parliament and Government;

2 the major government departments and the current Cabinet Ministers responsible for each one;

3 the ways in which the Commons and Lords can scrutinise and check up on the actions of government.

THE CABINET

The Cabinet usually meets once or twice a week. The meetings are chaired by the Prime Minister at 10 Downing Street. The job of the Cabinet is to co-ordinate government activity and the work of the civil service, and to decide on present and future policies. The Prime Minister usually takes a dominant role at Cabinet meetings, deciding on the agenda and summing up the feeling of the meeting at the end (votes rarely occur).

Hodder & Stoughton   *© 1994 Paul Higginson. The publishers grant permission for multiple copies of this sheet to be made in the place of purchase for use solely in that institution.*

The House of Commons

Briefly read through these questions, then watch Question Time and note down your answers.

1 What are the major roles of the Speaker?

2 Where do Government and Opposition leaders sit?

3 Where do Liberal Democrats and minor parties sit?

4 What is the significance of the two lines on the floor on either side of the central table?

5 How do MPs refer to one another and why is this terminology used?

6 How many questions did the Leader of the Opposition ask and what was the subject matter?

7 Give three reasons why a question might be asked (apart from simply to gain information)?

8 Supplementary questions which follow the original question are often very difficult to answer, Why?

9 Sometimes a Prime Minister might arrange for one of his backbenchers to ask a 'planted' question. Did this happen?

10 What was the best question you heard and why?

11 Which side did you feel performed best and why?

12 Question Time helps to make the Government more accountable. How?

13 Were there any aspects of the MPs' behaviour that surprised you?

14 Note one advantage and one disadvantage of televising the Commons.

Hodder & Stoughton   © *1994 Paul Higginson. The publishers grant permission for multiple copies of this sheet to be made in the place of purchase for use solely in that institution.*

Worksheet 2
Debate

Before a law is made the Government will publish a Green paper (a discussion document for interested parties to examine) and a White Paper (the Bill in draft form). After discussion, and changes if necessary, the Bill is presented to the Commons and goes through seven stages.

1 **First Reading:** the Bill is read out in the Commons.

2 **Second Reading:** discussion of the general principles of the Bill.

3 **Committee stage:** detailed discussion of every aspect by a small group of MPs.

4 **Report stage:** the Committee reports back to the House and amendments are made.

5 **Third Reading:** final discussion and vote.

6 **House of Lords:** peers suggest amendments to Bill.

7 **Royal Assent:** the Queen signs Bill, and it becomes an Act of Parliament.

Divide the class into two sections - Government and Opposition. Decide who is to occupy the key positions such as Prime Minister, Leader of the Opposition, Home Secretary and Shadow Home Affairs Spokesperson. Students who are not in the Cabinet or Shadow Cabinet become backbench MPs. The Government has introduced a Bill to reduce the legal drinking age to 16, and the Bill has reached its Second Reading in the Commons. Government spokespersons must work out arguments for the Bill, and Opposition parties arguments against. Try to find out what the law is in other countries.

During the debate remember the following points of Parliamentary procedure.

1 All speeches/points are made through the Speaker (the teacher) who chairs the debate and calls on MPs to speak.

2 You may only speak when asked to by the Speaker - stand up when you make a speech.

3 The Speaker is referred to as Mr Speaker or Madam Speaker, and fellow MPs as My Honourable Friend. The Prime Minister, the Leader of the Opposition, members and ex-members of the Cabinet are called My Right Honourable Friend.

4 The Home Secretary will make the first speech, followed by the Shadow Home Affairs Spokesperson, then other MPs will make points if called by the Speaker.

5 At the end of the debate the Home Secretary and his Shadow will briefly sum up before the final vote takes place.

Hodder & Stoughton

© *1994 Paul Higginson. The publishers grant permission for multiple copies of this sheet to be made in the place of purchase for use solely in that institution.*

Worksheet 3
Freelandia - Crisis in Cabinet

1 Each member of the class is allocated a position in Cabinet (Prime Minister, Foreign Secretary, Chancellor of the Exchequer, Defence Secretary, etc.). The teacher is the Cabinet Secretary - a senior civil servant.

2 Freelandia is a small country in West Africa. Formerly a British colony it is now independent with a US-style constitution, free elections and a vigorous economy. Although it is a poor, developing country it has a thriving market economy and close political and economic links with the UK (although only a handful of British citizens live there). Oil (exported to Europe) is the most important source of revenue. Freelandia has two large but poor neighbours: Africansa, a left-wing dictatorship and Islamia, ruled by a powerful religious leader. Freelandia and Africansa have been in dispute for many years over their border. Africansa says that part of its territory was given to Freelandia when it gained independence. Freelandia denies this and has built new towns and settlements in the disputed territory.

3 The Cabinet receives intelligence reports that Africansa forces have invaded Freelandia, imprisoned the Prime Minister and taken over the running of the country. Its superior military forces have overwhelmed the tiny Freelandia army and the country is now under complete Africansa control.

4 You must now decide what action to take. The Prime Minister will chair the meeting but all members of the Cabinet will be expected to contribute. The Cabinet Secretary will update you with news as it comes in, and will provide you with information - he/she will not, however, be able to take part in decision making.

5 At the end of the meeting, draft a short press release containing your proposals for action.

To be given out by the Cabinet Secretary at appropriate moments during the simulation:

✂————————————————————————————————

UN calls for an emergency meeting 'to resolve the problem peacefully'.

✂————————————————————————————————

Military commanders say 'casualties will be high' if force is used.

✂————————————————————————————————

Neighbouring Islamia supports the new government of Freelandia and says it will intervene 'to resist any Western imperialist aggression'.

✂————————————————————————————————

The US President says 'British intervention would be unhelpful - the countries involved must sort out their difficulties for themselves'.

✂————————————————————————————————

Africansa agrees to withdraw but only on condition that it keeps the disputed territory.

✂————————————————————————————————

An opinion poll in *The Times* shows that 60 per cent of British people support the use of force by UK 'to liberate Freelandia'.

✂————————————————————————————————

Twenty British hostages are taken and threatened. The BBC reports stories of atrocities by Africansa troops on civilians in Freelandia.

✂————————————————————————————————

The headline in *The Guardian* says 'People of Freelandia organise resistance to occupation ¨ request British help'.

✂————————————————————————————————

The Opposition party in the UK calls for the mobilisation of a task force to liberate Freelandia. The Leader of the Opposition says 'aggression can never be rewarded'.

✂————————————————————————————————

Intelligence reports confirm that Islamia has developed its own nuclear bomb.

Hodder & Stoughton

© 1994 Paul Higginson. The publishers grant permission for multiple copies of this sheet to be made in the place of purchase for use solely in that institution.

4 Public Spending

CENTRAL GOVERNMENT

PUBLIC SPENDING

Central government spends a great deal of money. In 1993-4, £276 billion were allocated to the various government departments. Social Security received the largest share, almost £60m (for unemployment, sickness and child benefit, pensions, etc.). Local government was next with £59 billion, followed by Health (£29m) and Defence (£24m).

These are the approximate percentage figures for each department. 'Local Government' includes Education, Social Services and the Police. 'Others' includes the Home Office (£2.5bn), Employment (£3.4bn), Reserve (£4bn), EC (£1.4bn), Nationalised Industries (£3.8bn), Housing (£2.8bn), Overseas Development (£2.3bn), Agriculture (£3bn), Transport (£2.7bn), Legal Departments (£2.7bn).

Activities

1 For each government department above write down three ways money is spent, for example Social Security ¨ pensions, income support, maternity benefit.

2 If you were Chancellor of the Exchequer how would you share out the cake? Which departments would you cut and who would get extra money?

3 What kind of things might the Reserve be spent on?

TAXES

The Government raises most of this money through various forms of taxation.

There are essentially three types of tax.

1 Taxes on income. These include income tax (paid by most of those in work), corporation tax (paid by companies out of their profits), and National Insurance which is paid by employees and employers to help pay for benefits (like pensions and unemployment).

2 Taxes on spending. Value Added Tax (VAT) is a tax on goods and services (certain things like food and children's clothes are currently exempt). Duties are paid on petrol, alcohol and tobacco and on certain goods entering the country.

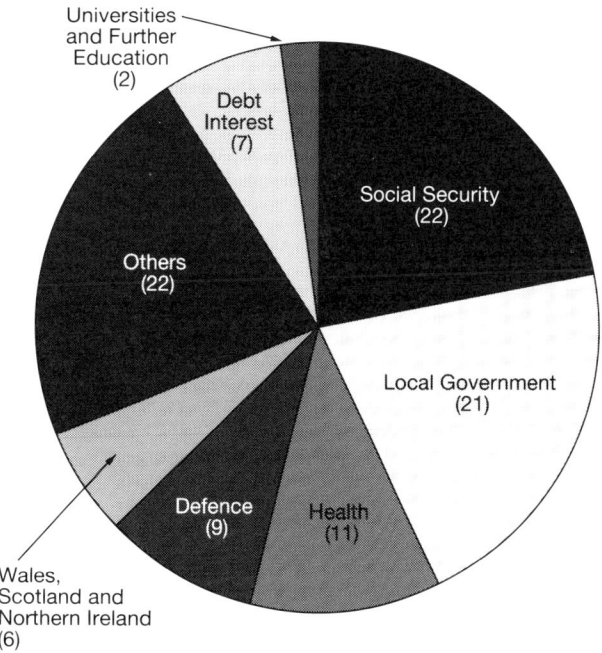

Public spending in the UK, 1993-4 (%)

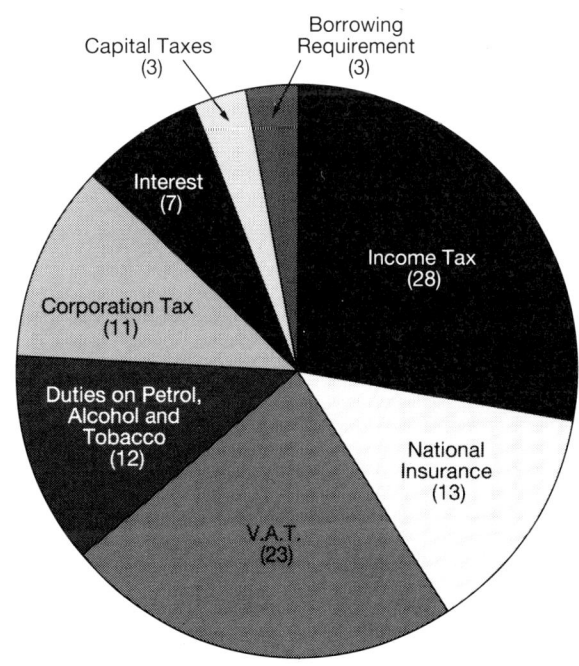

Forms of taxation in the UK, 1993-4 (%)

Hodder & Stoughton   © 1994 Paul Higginson. The publishers grant permission for multiple copies of this sheet to be made in the place of purchase for use solely in that institution.

3 Taxes on capital The government taxes wealth. When individuals sell assets such as property, shares or antiques any profit or gain is taxed. Exemptions are granted on certain assets such as a person's home (but not on second homes). Furthermore, any capital transfers such as gifts, or money inherited on death, are also liable to tax.

■ Activities

1 Find out the current rates of income tax and VAT.

2 Find out the difference between a progressive and a regressive tax, and between direct and indirect tax.

3 In recent opinion polls a majority of voters indicated that they would prefer higher taxes and better public services rather than lower taxes but worse services. What is your view?

4 Comment on and discuss the following statements:-

"People who earn a lot like film-stars and top businessmen should pay a very high rate of tax."

"The government should not tax people when they die. Their assets should all go to their families."

"The government could help save lives by dramatically increasing the tax on cigarettes. It could also cut down on the number of cars on our roads (reducing traffic congestion and pollution) by increasing road and petrol taxes."

THE BUDGET

The Plans for the raising and spending of money are contained in the annual Budget. This is prepared by the Treasury in the form of a Finance Bill. The Chancellor of the Exchequer outlines the main proposals to the Commons in his Budget Speech.

DIFFERENCES BETWEEN LOCAL AND CENTRAL GOVERNMENT

	Central Government	Local Government
1 Located in	Whitehall, London	Local town hall/civic offices
2 Consists of	Ministers (MPs or Lords) led by Prime Minister	Councillors in Ruling Group headed by Council Leader
3 Elected every	Five years	Four years
4 Electoral area	Constituency	Ward
5 Approximate turnout in elections	75%	40%
6 Advised/assisted by	Civil servants in departments	Local government officers in departments
7 Administrative structure	Departments e.g. (Defence, Agriculture) headed by Minister	Committees e.g. (Planning, Transportation, Education) led by Chairperson

Hodder & Stoughton
© 1994 Paul Higginson. The publishers grant permission for multiple copies of this sheet to be made in the place of purchase for use solely in that institution.

ORGANISATION AND FUNCTIONS OF LOCAL GOVERNMENT

Central government runs the country, dealing with all the major national issues like defence, foreign affairs, the economy, etc. Local government is concerned with local issues such as refuse collection, local planning and libraries. However, local government is subservient to the decisions of central government and most laws concerned with local government are made by Parliament. Local councils can only make laws on very minor matters such as dogs fouling the streets - these are called by-laws. In recent years, central government has increased its control over local government, and local councils have lost much of their independence. Most of the country has a two-tier system of local government: large county councils which control major issues (police and fire services, main roads, education, social services, refuse disposal), and smaller district councils for more local matters (minor roads, refuse collection, local planning). If you live in one of the big metropolitan cities or London there is only one tier of local government, which does everything. Scotland, Wales and Northern Ireland have two-tier systems.

HOW LOCAL COUNCILS GET THEIR MONEY

1 Grants are fixed by central government.

2 Business Rates are paid by factories, shop, offices, etc. at a rate fixed by central government.

3 Council Tax is a property tax paid by all householders, with a 25 per cent reduction for people living alone. Those on low incomes are exempt.

4 Other sources are borrowing, council house rents, entrance charges for swimming pools, etc.

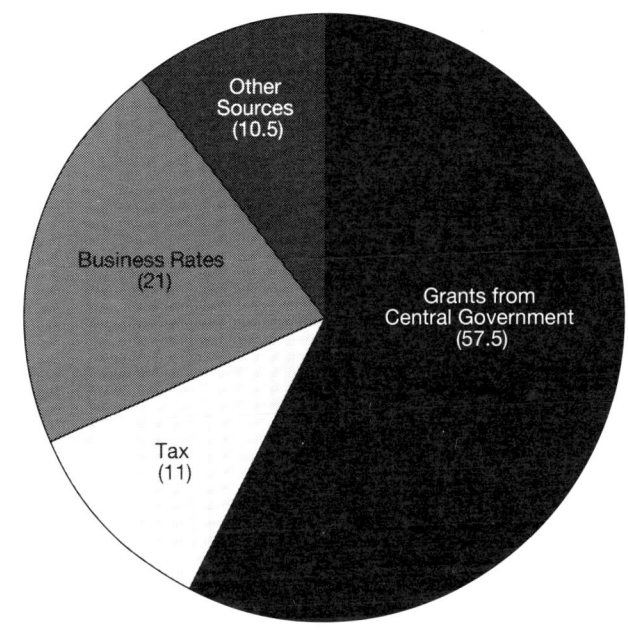

Sources of income for local government, 1992 (%)

HOW THE MONEY IS SPENT

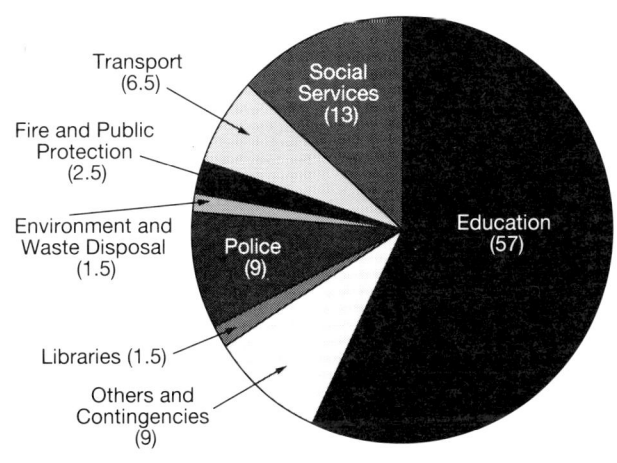

Hertfordshire County Council spending in 1992-3 (%)

■ Activities

1 Find out:

a) The name of your local council, and whether it is one-tier or two-tier.

b) How much your local tax was last year (you or your parents may have received leaflets on this) and what services your local council provides.

c) Ways in which central government has recently reduced the powers of local government, for example capping, opting-out, competitive tendering, the abolition of the GLC, sale of council houses, etc.

2 Invite a local councillor into class to explain his or her work.

3 Attend the next meeting of the council at your local town hall.

Hodder & Stoughton

© 1994 Paul Higginson. The publishers grant permission for multiple copies of this sheet to be made in the place of purchase for use solely in that institution.

Below are two outlines for a class debate concerning public expenditure. Read through the extracts below to get some basic ideas, then divide into two groups (one for and one against) and prepare further points to strengthen your case. Decide who will open and close the debate, who will speak and what points you will make. Keep your speeches fairly short and allow as many people as possible to have a say.

THE MONARCHY - A WASTE OF TAXPAYERS' MONEY

For

"The Queen is the richest woman in the world with a personal fortune of £7billion. Despite this wealth she receives £8m from the taxpayer each year, as well as money for the upkeep of her royal castles, the royal yacht Britannia and several aircraft of the Queen's Flight (total cost to the taxpayer £20m per annum). We also have to subsidise the other royal hangers-on to the tune of another £2m per annum. The Royal Family embodies and helps to preserve a class-based society based on elitism, snobbery, the hereditary principle and outdated traditions. In a modern democracy the head of state should be an elected President."

Against

"The Queen is good value for money. She promotes trade and tourism and sells Britain overseas. She advises the Prime Minister, is Head of the Commonwealth and because she has no political allegiance she can rise above party politics, unify the nation in times of crisis and protect our constitutional democracy from dictatorship. Most opinion polls indicate that she is immensely popular and good at her job. A nation needs a figurehead, a symbol of national unity, a link with its history and tradition - an elected President could never achieve this."

DEFENCE SPENDING SHOULD BE HALVED AND THE MONEY SAVED SPENT ON THE HEALTH SERVICE

For

"Our defence spending as a proportion of national income is the highest in Western Europe at 5 per cent. Our economic competitors have much lower rates: France 4 per cent, West Germany 3 per cent, Japan 1 per cent. We spend almost as much on defence as we do on health. With the end of the Cold War and the collapse of communism there is no need to maintain defence spending at current levels. Cuts could be made in many areas: Fortress Falklands, an independent nuclear deterrent, commitments to NATO, the number of overseas bases, reduction in overall manpower. The money saved could be spent to help reduce NHS waiting lists and provide better medical care."

Against

"A strong defence policy stops war by acting as a deterrent. Britain is still a key player in world affairs as the Falklands and Gulf Wars prove. Maintaining an effective military force helps to preserve democracy and freedom in this country, and enables us to intervene in the world to assist countries like Kuwait which need our help. There is no point having a good education system or health service if we are unable to defend it. Furthermore, the defence industry provides a much-needed boost to our economy; cuts would lead to a big increase in unemployment."

Hodder & Stoughton

© 1994 Paul Higginson. The publishers grant permission for multiple copies of this sheet to be made in the place of purchase for use solely in that institution.

Worksheet 2
The Local Council

As members of Hillshire County Council you must agree to cuts in this year's budget. The grant you receive from central government has been reduced so you must slice £20m from your total budget of £450m. At present the budget looks like this: Education £240m, Social Services £100m, Highways/Waste Disposal £70m, others £40m.

Divide into three committees - Education, Social Services and Highways - and prepare to argue your case in the Council Meeting. Below are possible cuts:

	Saving
1 Education	
Increase class sizes by 10 per cent losing 250 teachers.	£5m
Amalgamate three small high schools into one large college.	£3m
Cut all nursery education for under fives.	£5m
Increase school meal charges by 25 per cent.	£1m
Scrap the Careers Guidance Service.	£2m
2 Social Services	
Cut 20 per cent of all social workers - 150 jobs.	£3m
Close three day centres for elderly and disabled people.	£2m
Close down a residential home for mentally ill people and place the residents in the community.	£2m
3 Highways and Waste Disposal	
Suspend all non-emergency road maintenance for one year.	£2m
Scrap a much-needed one-way system in a major town centre (planned to alleviate chronic congestion).	£2m
Collect refuse every two weeks instead of every week.	£2m
Halve the number of street-cleaners.	£1m
4 Other possibilities	
Cut the opening hours of all libraries by 50 per cent.	£1m
Scrap a plan to build a new leisure centre.	£1.5m
Make OAPs pay full fare on public transport.	£1.5m
Close a very popular local museum.	£1m

Argue your corner - but remember agreement must eventually be reached for a total of £20m in cuts. If no consensus emerges from the discussion then the cuts must be made by a series of votes on each proposal.

Hodder & Stoughton

© 1994 Paul Higginson. The publishers grant permission for multiple copies of this sheet to be made in the place of purchase for use solely in that institution.

Worksheet 3
Local Taxation

Local councils now get approximately 11 per cent of their money from local people, and in recent years three main methods of taxation have been used to collect this revenue.

THE RATES

Each property is valued and the householder is taxed. The greater the value of the property the higher the tax. **Advantages:** it is easy to understand and calculate, it is cheap to collect, it is very difficult to avoid, there are rebates for those on low income, it is linked to ability to pay. **Disadvantages:** it is regressive (takes a larger proportion from those on a low income, although rate rebates rectify this), buildings, not people, are taxed (so a single person pays as much as four adults next door), it is a disincentive to property improvement.

THE POLL TAX OR COMMUNITY CHARGE

Introduced in 1989, this was an equal tax on each adult over 18 regardless of property or income. Those on income support, and students, paid only 20 per cent of the charge. **Advantages:** It is fair - everyone pays something (only a third of voters paid full rates), so it makes councils more accountable for their actions and less spendthrift, it should lead to lower tax bills as councils strive to save money, it is simple (everyone pays equal amounts for equal services). **Disadvantages:** it is unfair (it is a flat rate tax not linked to ability to pay), it is expensive to collect (£1.5m a year), it is easy to avoid (it resulted in thousands leaving the electoral roll).

THE COUNCIL TAX

Introduced in 1993. Each house is placed in one of eight bands based on its market value. The householder pays the tax, and the amount remains the same if there are two or twenty people living in the house. A reduction of 25 per cent applies to someone living alone, and people on low incomes receive a full rebate. Discounts also apply to full time students,

Band	Value of Property	Ratio of Tax Bill
A	less than £40,000	0.67
B	£40,000 - £52,000	0.78
C	£52,000 - £68,000	0.89
D	£68,000 - £88,000	1.00
E	£88,000 - £120,000	1.22
F	£120,000 - £160,000	1.44
G	£160,000 - £320,000	1.67
H	£320,000 +	2.00

apprentices, student nurses, Youth Training trainees and severely mentally impaired people. The ratio of tax bill refers to the proportion each householder pays, for example someone in Band A will pay two-thirds of the Band D rate (Band D is the average charge). The Council Tax is based on three factors: it is a mixture of rates (it is a property tax), the poll tax (it takes account of the number of adults in the house, i.e. the discount for sole occupants), it is based on income (the poor receive full rebates)

❑ Questions

1 Using the information provided, list the advantages and disadvantages of the Council Tax.

2 Rates enabled the majority of people in local elections to vote to 'spend other people's money' (Nicholas Ridley, Conservative Environment Secretary). Do you agree?

3 'Everyone who uses council services like roads and street lights should pay the same flat rate.' What do you think of this viewpoint - give reasons.

4 Some politicians would like to see local taxation abolished and replaced by a larger central government grant. What would be the implications of this proposal?

5 Liberal Democrats are campaigning for a local income tax to replace the Council Tax. This would come out of a person's pay packet in the same way that income tax is deducted by central government. List the pros and cons of such a measure.

Hodder & Stoughton

© 1994 Paul Higginson. The publishers grant permission for multiple copies of this sheet to be made in the place of purchase for use solely in that institution.

5 Pressure Groups

Pressure groups are organisations that try to influence decision makers. By putting pressure on local and central government, MPs, political parties, civil servants and the general public, they hope to achieve their objectives. Greenpeace, for example, wants the government to change its policies on dumping sewage in the North Sea. Other pressure groups might want to resist changes - the Campaign for Real Ale (CAMRA) is trying to preserve traditional methods of beer-making and stop the big brewing companies from changing the character of the British pub. Unlike political parties, pressure groups do not put forward candidates for election or try to gain political office directly.

Most political scientists categorise pressure groups into two main types - sectional and cause.

Sectional groups protect the interests of their members, usually a small section of society. Examples are trade unions (National Union of Mineworkers) and professional associations (British Medical Association). A year's subscription for these pressure groups can be quite expensive but the member may gain many benefits, perhaps preventing a pay cut, or negotiating better working conditions.

Cause groups promote a particular cause which they hope will be good for the whole of society (not just their members). Examples are Campaign for Nuclear Disarmament (CND), OXFAM, and Friends of the Earth. Many of these pressure groups are registered charities and if there is an annual subscription it is usually very small.

■ Activities

1 Write down the aims of the following pressure groups and then classify them as sectional or cause: NUS; NFU; MIND; Bar Council; UNISON; Shelter; Howard League; TGWU; AA; RSPCA; Lord's Day Observance Society; Ramblers' Association; Life; CBI.

2 Add any other groups to your list that you know and share these with the rest of the class.

3 In general, which groups do you think will be most successful in influencing government policy ¨ sectional or cause? Give reasons for your answer.

4 Some political scientists categorise pressure groups into insider and outsider groups. **Insider groups** are on friendly terms with the government and are regularly consulted by Ministers, for example, the NFU. **Outsider groups** have little direct influence with the Government and are generally kept at arm's length by Ministers. They have to rely on indirect methods of pressure like demonstrations, petitions, and the use of the mass media. A typical outsider group is Greenpeace. Go through your list again, writing Insider or Outsider by each group.

How do pressure groups pressurise? What methods do they use to achieve their aims? Study the following extracts taken from leaflets issued by two cause groups - Amnesty International and Christian CND.

Hodder & Stoughton   *© 1994 Paul Higginson. The publishers grant permission for multiple copies of this sheet to be made in the place of purchase for use solely in that institution.*

Amnesty International

...a worldwide movement which is independent of any government, political faction, ideology, economic interest, or religious creed. Its activities focus strictly on prisoners:

- it seeks the release of prisoners of conscience. These are men and women detained anywhere for their beliefs, colour, sex, ethnic origin, language or religion who have neither used nor advocated violence
- it advocates fair and early trials for all political prisoners and works on behalf of such people detained without charge or without trial
- it opposes the death penalty and torture or other cruel, inhuman or degrading treatment or punishment of all prisoners without reservation

How does it work?

When news of an arrest reaches Amnesty, the facts are examined to establish if the victim is a prisoner of conscience. The case is then 'adopted' by one of the worldwide network of Amnesty groups. Letters are sent to governments, embassies, leading newspapers and the prisoner's family and friends. In addition, members organise public meetings and arrange special publicity events, such as vigils at embassies. They collect signatures for international petitions and raise money to send relief, such as medicine, food and clothing, to the prisoners and their families. In the case of prisoners facing torture or the death penalty, Amnesty International uses an Urgent Action Scheme which generates a flood of telegrams and express letters to the appropriate government authorities.

Write a letter

Take part in Amnesty's Letter Writing Campaign " each edition of our magazine 'Amnesty' carries details of prisoners in need of help. They may be facing execution, be ill or have been detained for a prolonged period in severe conditions. Send special letters or cards on behalf of these prisoners to government authorities as proof of the mounting weight if public opinion.

Join a Group

If you want to take a more active part in Amnesty's work then join one of the British Section's 294 groups. All groups adopt individual prisoners and take part in campaigns which focus public attention on specific patterns of human rights violations. Local groups represent Amnesty in the community and contribute to the financing of the organisation through fund-raising activities.

Send a Donation

Researching into the identities and conditions of individual prisoners, sending observers to trials, supporting prisoners' families, preparing and publishing reports are all essential but expensive. For Amnesty to survive and expand its work, your financial help is urgently needed.

Christian C.N.D.

Many Christians, of all denominations and walks of life, feel that the time has come for them to bear witness against the shadow of nuclear weapons. From this conviction has grown the Christian Campaign for Nuclear Disarmament.

Just as it is difficult to be a Christian by yourself, so it is also difficult for you to work for peace and disarmament without others. You can get in touch with others by joining CND or another peace organisation. There will probably be a local group of some kind in your area as well, or perhaps with others you could help to start a group in your church community. Being in a group is a way of showing publicly your commitment, as well as creating a community from which activity, worship and hope can spring. But even if you are on your own you can keep informed and help to inform others in your church, locality and family.

You can remind church organisations, leaders and government about their responsibilities and about issues. You can try to bring your concern to the attention of the media and into your worship, to make that concern grow. You can also with others in Christian CND proclaim your beliefs and witness to peace by taking part in acts of witness, vigils, demonstrations, etc. Christian CND can provide you with opportunities to make your voice heard, and resources to inform and encourage discussion.

❑ Questions

1   List the methods used by these two groups.

2   Do you think that they will be successful in achieving their goals? Give reasons for your answer.

3   What other methods of influence might a group use?

Hodder & Stoughton   © 1994 Paul Higginson. The publishers grant permission for multiple copies of this sheet to be made in the place of purchase for use solely in that institution.

TRADE UNIONS

Trade Unions are a particular type of sectional pressure group. Many of you will join a trade union when you start work. The main purpose of unions is to negotiate with employers over pay and conditions. Clearly, if workers join together in a union they will have greater influence and power than one employee on his or her own. About half of all trade unions are affiliated to the Labour party. Three quarters of Labour's funding comes from the unions and the unions have great influence on party policy. One in three workers is a member of a trade union and most unions are affiliated to the Trades Union Congress (TUC). Some of these unions are general unions representing workers from many different industries, for example, the Transport and General Workers Union. Others represent a particular industry or profession, for example, National Union of Teachers.

❏ Questions

1 Unions are not just about getting a good pay deal. Study the UNISON advertisement and note the other things a trade union might do for a member.

UNISON delivers protection

Whatever your grade, you can't protect your job and improve your pay and conditions without the backing of a strong union.
With over 850,000 members working in local government, UNISON is the most effective union in local government. And because we are one of the biggest unions on the pay negotiating bodies, we have a major say when it comes to reaching agreements with your employer.

Working in local government can throw up all kinds of difficult problems. Whether it's an issue affecting you and your colleagues, such as cuts in services or redundancies or the reorganisation of your authority, or an issue that concerns just you, such as regrading, or a grievance, UNISON has the time, resources and know-how to get the best solutions.

No matter what job you do there's always someone there to help you if you have problems at work. UNISON has more workplace stewards and representatives than any other union in the country. This is backed up by experienced national and regional full-time officers, dealing exclusively with local government.

And if you have a problem at work there's our guaranteed high standard of advice, representation and professional help when and where you need it on, for example, health and safety, new technology or Compulsory Competitive Tendering.

UNISON delivers democracy

You and your colleagues are in the driving seat of every area of UNISON's work, because you elect the people you want to speak for you at every level of the union, from the workplace to the National Executive - you will have a major say on the issues that directly concern you.

A fair commitment to fair representation and equal opportunities for all is at the heart of UNISON, giving women in particular the voice they need at every level of the union.

And UNISON will keep you right up-to-date with what's happening. Your own regular magazine, delivered directly to you and specifically written for members in local government, brings you up-to-the-minute information about the union and the service you work in.

2 During the Thatcher Government (1979 to 1990) trade union membership fell by approximately 25 per cent from 13m to under 10m. Suggest reasons for this.

✪ Further study

1 Write off to a pressure group (some addresses are given on page 93). Find out: a) the type of group, its origins and history; b) its objectives; c) the methods it uses; d) whether or not it has been successful in achieving its goals. Bring this information into class to discuss with others.

2 Invite a member of a pressure group or trade union to talk to the class.

3 Investigate the links that trade unions have with the Labour Party (addresses are given at the end of the book) and find out how these have changed in the 1990s.

Hodder & Stoughton   © 1994 Paul Higginson. The publishers grant permission for multiple copies of this sheet to be made in the place of purchase for use solely in that institution.

The Superstore

It has been proposed that a new Safebury's superstore be built on Little Meadows, a greenfield site midway between two towns with very poor shopping facilities. In a recent newspaper survey, 65 per cent of local people wanted a new store in the area.

Several pressure groups are involved.

1 Friends of the Earth "The superstore will cause tremendous environmental damage to the area. Little Meadows will be buried under concrete and large areas of woodland will be lost forever. The land is also a breeding ground for a rare species of owl."

2 Safebury's Ltd. "There is no superstore in this area and local people need and want our store. No sites are suitable within the town and this is the best greenfield site as it lies midway between the two communities. We have researched other greenfield sites but Little Meadow is easily the best spot in terms of geographical, engineering and construction factors."

3 Construction Workers' and Shop Workers' Union "This project will create hundreds of jobs in an unemployment blackspot. Many will be employed on the construction of the building and new roads; and of course shopworkers will be needed when the store opens."

4 Association of Small Shopkeepers "This store will put many of our members out of business. The corner shop plays a vital role in the local community but we can't compete with the major supermarket chains. There are plenty of small shops in the area ¨ we don't need Safeburys."

5 Little Meadows Local Residents' Association "The store will spoil our views of beautiful countryside and will bring down the value of our houses. The peace and tranquillity of this delightful spot will be destroyed and our roads will be clogged with heavy-goods vehicles and cars."

6 Confederation of British Industry "Our study of this area shows that massive investment is required to boost the local economy and create jobs. If the Safebury's project is a success other businesses will follow and the whole region could be revitalised."

A Public Inquiry has been set up to examine the arguments and take evidence from the pressure groups concerned.

THE INQUIRY

1 Get into seven groups. One group represents the Public Inquiry team. The other six represent the pressure groups.

2 The Public Inquiry team writes down questions to ask the different pressure groups.

3 Members of the six pressure groups must put their case to the Inquiry. Decide how you are going to present your arguments (five to ten minutes per pressure group).

4 When the evidence has been submitted, a general debate can take place between all parties. How will you respond to criticism from other pressure groups?

5 Finally the Inquiry must reach a verdict, through discussion and, if necessary, a final vote.

Hodder & Stoughton   © 1994 *Paul Higginson. The publishers grant permission for multiple copies of this sheet to be made in the place of purchase for use solely in that institution.*

Trade Union Terminology

Find out the meaning of each of the following terms and write it in the space provided. Compare your answers with those of other members of the group.

1 Strike

2 Closed Shop

3 Arbitration

4 Shop Steward

5 Picketing

6 Secondary Picketing

7 Redundancy

8 General Secretary

9 Free-collective bargaining

10 Sequestration

11 Winter of Discontent

12 Political Levy

13 White-collar union

Hodder & Stoughton

© 1994 Paul Higginson. The publishers grant permission for multiple copies of this sheet to be made in the place of purchase for use solely in that institution.

Worksheet 3
Strike!

Discovery PLC makes personal stereos. This is an extract from a letter that the company has just written to all its 200 employees:

"Because of high wages paid to our workforce our products are too expensive and we cannot compete with cheaper foreign imports. Unfortunately, we will have to cut wages by 25 per cent to survive ¨ the alternative is to make a quarter of all staff redundant. We hope that you will all understand our reluctance to lay off workers and our preference for an across-the-board pay cut."

1   Divide the class in two: half represents the management (Board of Directors), and half the workers (Shop Stewards).

2   Workers' instructions: a) Elect a chairperson or chief negotiator. b) Discuss the letter and decide on what action to take. Note that if strike action is to take place a majority of the workers must agree by means of a secret ballot. (for purposes of the role play assume that the shop stewards represent the whole workforce of 200 employees.)

3   Management's instructions: a) Elect a Chairperson of the Board. b) The local press printed the following headline yesterday: 'Unions say strike is possible - Discovery in wage dispute'. Discuss a strategy to deal with any tactic the union may use (take votes on decisions ¨ the chairperson has the casting vote).

4   Both sides may arrange to meet at any time. This must be done through the Personnel Officer (the teacher). During these meetings any side can have time out to discuss tactics amongst themselves.

STRIKE! - SHOP STEWARDS' VIEWPOINTS

Cut out and distribute these to workers where necessary during the initial discussion.

1   *"I can't afford a cut in wages. High wages aren't to blame - it's the fact that the company won't install new machinery and produce new products. It's management's fault."*

2   *"I agree with management. Our high wages cause our products to be over-priced compared with our competitors. I can't afford to be made redundant. I want an agreement to reduce wages."*

3   *"I haven't been here long and I need a job. If lower wages save jobs then I'll consider them."*

4   *"We should ask to see the profit figures. We need more information from the company. How do we know management is telling the truth?"*

5   *"Maybe we can find a solution that saves jobs but doesn't cut wages. Perhaps we could cut other costs like expensive cars and executive lunches for the bosses."*

6   *"Maybe we could work out a productivity agreement - we could agree to work harder and produce more."*

7   *"We've got to threaten management with a strike, otherwise they'll walk all over us. We've got to make a stand on this."*

8   *"They are bluffing - we must strike. I read in the paper yesterday that they are going to make big profits this year."*

9   *"If we stick together we'll win. If we strike for a few days they'll back down and we can reach a compromise."*

10 *"I'll never get another job if I'm made redundant. I can't keep my kids on my wages. We may have to go on strike."*

Hodder & Stoughton   © 1994 Paul Higginson. The publishers grant permission for multiple copies of this sheet to be made in the place of purchase for use solely in that institution.

Worksheet 4

Strike!

Cut out and distribute these to workers where necessary during time out huddles.

✂--

Latest Press release: 'Record Profits at Discovery'

✂--

Your General Secretary and National Union Executive send you the following telegram: 'We advise strike action - we will support your case 100 per cent.'

✂--

Some workers are 'scabbing'. Write a letter to ALL the workers saying 100 per cent solidarity in the strike is necessary.

✂--

You have been asked to appear on the BBC's *Question Time*. Choose two people and work out what they will say.

✂--

A local TV station has given you five minutes on its news bulletin to present your side of the story. The bulletin goes out in ten minutes. Choose two people to go on TV and present your views. Decide what you are going to say.

✂--

Cut out and distribute to the management where necessary during time out huddles.

✂--

Secret letter from the National President of your company: We have decided to introduce new machinery at your plant. We MUST cut staff by 50 per cent. We can't afford high redundancy payments. Can we sack workers if they go on strike? Can we provoke workers to strike?

✂--

The TUC is supporting the workers. No union is willing to work at your plant. You are being blacked. People are refusing to buy your products. Can you reach a compromise with the workers?

✂--

Some workers are 'scabbing'. Write a letter to all the employees encouraging the 'scabs' and inviting the workers to leave the union and go back to work.

✂--

You have been asked to appear on the BBC's *Question Time*. Choose two people and work out what they will say.

✂--

A local TV station has given you five minutes on its news bulletin to present your side of the story. The bulletin goes out in ten minutes. Choose two people to go on TV and present your views. Decide what you are going to say.

✂--

Hodder & Stoughton

© 1994 Paul Higginson. The publishers grant permission for multiple copies of this sheet to be made in the place of purchase for use solely in that institution.

6 The Law

WHY DO WE NEED LAWS?

Laws are designed to make us act in a certain way (for example to stop at a red light or to respect other's property). If we break the law then we are penalised in some way (a fine, prison, etc.). Many laws are written down in Acts of Parliament, but most institutions (like schools, churches, or companies) and all sports and games also have rules which people obey.

■ Activities

1   Write down a list of school rules and say which you agree and which you disagree with.

2   What sanctions (punishments) might you receive if you break the rules? Are such sanctions too soft or too harsh?

3   Why are laws (and sanctions) necessary?

CIVIL & CRIMINAL LAW - WHAT'S THE DIFFERENCE?

	Civil Law	Criminal Law
Purpose?	Aims to redress private wrongs between individuals or individual organisations	Aims to uphold law and order on behalf of society in general
Who takes action?	The individual takes proceedings	The police prosecute through the Crown Prosecution Service
Where are cases heard? (in first instance)	County court and High Court '	Magistrates' court and Crown Court
Burden of proof	Balance of probabilities'	'Beyond reasonable doubt'
Action against wrongdoer	Compensation by payment of 'damages'	Punishment, e.g. fine, imprisonment, etc.

■ Activity

List the following cases under two headings - 'Civil Law' and 'Criminal Law'.

• murder	• divorce proceedings
• spraying graffiti on a railway bridge film	• avoiding paying the fare on a train
• actor taking action against a magazine for libel	• racial discrimination in a job interview
• using threatening and abusive language to a neighbour	• adoption of a child
	• drunk and disorderly
• failure of a company to honour a contract	• payment of maintenance
• dispute over a will	•exceeding the speed limit
• shoplifting	• company going bankrupt and unable to repay money it owes

Hodder & Stoughton

© 1994 Paul Higginson. The publishers grant permission for multiple copies of this sheet to be made in the place of purchase for use solely in that institution.

THE SYSTEM OF COURTS

Civil	County court	Minor cases and disputes over contracts which involve small amounts of damages.	Circuit judge
	High Court	More important cases and claims for large amounts of damages.	Judge (occasionally with jury)
Criminal	Magistrates' Court	Minor cases - up to six months' imprisonment or a small fine, probation, etc. Deals with 98 per cent of cases. For crimes leading to three to six months' prison, the accused can elect to go to Crown Court.	Unpaid, lay, JPs (Justice of the Peace) or occasionally Stipendiary Magistrate
	Crown Court	Serious cases - all cases resulting in over six months imprisonment & most cases leading to three to six months. Appeals from magistrates' court.	Judges or Recorders (barrister or solicitor); Jury, except for appeals from magistrates' court.
	Divisional Court of Queen's Bench	Takes appeals from magistrates' court on points of law in minor cases.	Lord Chief Justice and Judges
Civil and Criminal	Court of Appeal, Civil & Criminal Division	Appeals from lower courts (complex cases).	Three Appeal Judges
	House of Lords	Complex & significant cases from the Court of Appeal - highest Court in the land.	Law Lords (usually 5)

In addition the European Court of Justice (in Luxembourg) enforces EC laws and regulations, and the European Court of Human Rights (at Strasbourg) protects basic human rights across Europe.

❏ Questions

1 Given the choice, most people facing the possibility of three to six months' imprisonment choose to have their case heard in the Crown Court rather than the magistrates' court. Why is this?

2 Magistrates are ordinary men and women with no legal qualification who have undergone some basic training in the law. What are the advantages and disadvantages of having unpaid, part-time lay magistrates?

Hodder & Stoughton

© 1994 Paul Higginson. The publishers grant permission for multiple copies of this sheet to be made in the place of purchase for use solely in that institution.

❖ Discussion points

Make a list of the laws which are most frequently broken. Are there any laws that we should get rid of or amend in some way? Draw up arguments for and against the following proposals:

- reduce the drinking age in pubs from 18 to 16;
- legalise soft drugs;
- lower the homosexual age of consent to 16 (the same as for heterosexuals);
- restrict smoking to outdoors or in one's own home;
- raise the school leaving age to 17;
- decrease the voting age to 16;
- legalise prostitution;
- scrap the seat-belt laws.

WHO ARE THE JUDGES?

Judges are barristers or solicitors with long experience, appointed by the Queen on the advice of the Prime Minister and the Lord Chancellor (the head of the judiciary). It is important that they remain independent from politics and politicians, so once appointed they can remain in office until they are 75. It is almost impossible for the government to get rid of a judge it disagrees with. In theory, politicians make laws in Parliament and judges apply and enforce these laws. However Acts have to be interpreted and words or phrases in Acts can have many meanings. What, for example, does a police officer mean by 'reasonable' when he says 'reasonable force' or 'reasonable suspicion', and how will it vary from case to case? Moreover, judges also make the common law ¨ this is the body of general principles that has been built up over centuries as judges make their decisions. Judges are therefore a very important part of the state machinery and it is essential that they be impartial, independent and non-political. Study the following extract, which is critical of the present judiciary.

'Most judges come from upper or upper middle class backgrounds. They have generally attended public schools followed by Oxford or Cambridge University. They are almost exclusively white, male and elderly, sharing a common background and training which makes them conservative in outlook and Conservative politically. What they see as the public interest is very often the interests of their class. Consequently they are inevitably hostile to trade unions, squatters, socialists, indeed anyone who threatens the status quo of the Establishment. Out of touch with reality and unrepresentative of the general population, the British judiciary is in need of drastic reform.'

❑ Questions

1 Is it necessary for the judiciary to be representative of the general population (i.e. to include a proportional number of women, ethnic minorities, Labour supporters, etc.)?

2 Suggest possible reforms to the judiciary.

3 In the US some judges are elected. What are the advantages and disadvantages of this?

4 'We are all political animals, products of our socialisation process, with our own prejudices and opinions. No one can be truly impartial or independent.' Do you agree?

TRIAL BY JURY

A basic part of the British legal system is that a person's guilt should be decided by his peers - trial by jury. A jury consists of 12 ordinary people aged between 18 and 70. They are usually asked to sit in Crown Court cases. Their job is to listen to the evidence presented by the prosecution and defence and then to declare their verdict (the judge pronounces the sentence). The verdict must be either unanimous or a majority of not less than ten to two. If agreement is not reached, the judge orders a retrial.

Hodder & Stoughton   © 1994 Paul Higginson. The publishers grant permission for multiple copies of this sheet to be made in the place of purchase for use solely in that institution.

Examine the arguments below, for and against juries.

Advantages

- Juries are made up of ordinary men and women who reflect society at large and generally reach a common-sense verdict.
- Ordinary people get to participate in the judicial system, ensuring that justice is not only done, but appears to be done.
- Juries are unpaid.

Disadvantages

- Juries very often can't understand evidence in complex fraud or City crime cases like insider-dealing.
- Juries can be biased or prejudiced.
- Juries often produce widely-differing verdicts on similar cases in different parts of the country (for example juries are much more likely to acquit in inner cities than in rural areas).
- Cases often depend on the styles of the prosecution/defence lawyers, who can employ clever psychological and oratorical skills to sway juries. Similarly one or two vociferous members of the jury may dominate the others.

❑ Questions

1 What alternatives are there to trial by jury?

2 In Northern Ireland, alleged terrorists are tried before a judge only - there are no juries. Why is this?

3 Should there be an intelligence test for jury members?

Hodder & Stoughton
© 1994 Paul Higginson. The publishers grant permission for multiple copies of this sheet to be made in the place of purchase for use solely in that institution.

Write in the legal age when you can do the following:

1 vote in elections;

2 buy cigarettes;

3 have sexual intercourse (law applies only to girls);

4 drink alcohol in private (with consent of parents);

5 be held responsible for a crime;

6 stand as a candidate for council or Parliament;

7 marry without parents' consent;

8 have your own passport (if parents sign form);

9 have a homosexual relationship (boys only);

10 get a part-time job (not before 7.00 a.m. or after 7.00 p.m., 8 hours maximum on Saturdays, 2 hours maximum on Sundays/weekdays, etc.);

11 see an 'adult' film at the cinema (containing strong language, violence or sex);

12 enter a pub (but not to drink alcohol);

13 leave home and marry (with consent of parents);

14 go to prison;

15 drive a moped or motorcycle;

16 smoke in a public place;

17 buy fireworks

18 own an air rifle;

19 adopt children

20 be tried and convicted for a crime if the prosecution can prove you knew what you were doing was wrong.

❖ Discussion points

Do you think any of these ages should be changed? If so, why?

Do other countries have different age rules?

Which of these laws are most frequently broken, and why?

Hodder & Stoughton   *© 1994 Paul Higginson. The publishers grant permission for multiple copies of this sheet to be made in the place of purchase for use solely in that institution.*

Worksheet 2
Legal Terminology

Match up the terms with the definitions by putting a number in the box.

Solicitor	
Legal aid	
Bail	
Barrister	
Law Lords	
Magistrate (JP)	
Indictable offence	
Summons	
Community service	
Coroner	
Stipendiary Magistrate	
Summary offence	
Remand in custody	
Judicial review	
Juvenile court	
Sue	
Small claims court	
Jury	
Crown Prosecution Service	
Clerk of the Court	

1 Money provided by the state for people on low incomes to pay legal expenses in certain cases.

2 Investigates sudden, violent or unnatural deaths.

3 Lawyer who is qualified to represent clients and plead cases in higher courts.

4 To begin a civil action.

5 Punishment involving a number of hours working in society (e.g. painting an old people's home, helping handicapped people).

6 Lawyer who gives legal advice and prepares cases for court. Often seen in magistrates' courts.

7 Twelve people (electors) who listen to evidence in court and decide whether a person is guilty or innocent.

8 Unpaid lay person with no legal qualification who sits in lower criminal courts.

9 A sum of money given as security so the accused can be released (he or she has to reappear later).

10 Lawyers who prosecute on behalf of the police in criminal cases.

11 Wrongdoing which is punishable by three months' imprisonment or more (the accused may claim trial by jury).

12 A barrister of at least seven years' standing who sits in lower criminal courts in London and large towns.

13 A qualified official (usually a solicitor) who advises JPs on points of law in the magistrates court.

14 Judicial scrutiny of the decisions of politicians to see if laws are being broken.

15 A quick, cheap, informal court system to deal with minor cases.

16 Hold the accused to await trial.

17 Court for young people (aged 10 to 17).

18 Written order to appear in court.

19 Minor wrongdoing which can be dealt with in the magistrates' court.

20 Members of the House of Lords who hear appeals.

Hodder & Stoughton   © 1994 Paul Higginson. The publishers grant permission for multiple copies of this sheet to be made in the place of purchase for use solely in that institution.

Mr Adams was shot and killed, late one evening, while alone in his detached house. His neighbour, Mr Brent, is arrested the next morning at home, charged with murder and is eventually brought before the Crown Court.

The class simulates the trial with the following characters:

Judge	This part could be taken by the teacher. He or she presides over the Court and passes sentence.
Prosecution and Defence barristers	You need at least two people, one for each side. They present evidence and question witnesses.
Jury	Made up of 12 men and women. A foreman is elected to chair its discussion.
Mr Brent	He maintains he is innocent, though he admits the gun used was his. He claims he spent the evening at home drinking with Mr Goss. Next morning, when arrested, tests proved Mr Brent had been drinking the previous evening.

Witnesses for the prosecution

PC Cox	He is convinced he saw Mr Brent running from the scene, though he was unable to catch him and it was dark.
Mrs Davies	She claims that Mr Adams and Mr Brent had argued fiercely the week before over money owed to Mr Brent by Mr Adams.
Mr Evans	He is a drinking partner of Mr Brent; he claims that the accused often got violent after drinking. He claims he visited Mr Brent on the evening of the murder but found no one at home.

Witnesses for the defence

Mrs Ford	She is Mr Brent's cleaner; she claims that the accused told her his gun had been stolen three days before the murder.
Mr Goss	He claims to have spent the whole evening of the murder drinking with the accused in his home.
Mr Harris	A friend of Mr Adams. Claims that Mr Adams owed money to a considerable number of people and had a number of enemies due to some rather shady business deals.

Although witnesses can embellish their evidence to a certain extent they must not deviate from the general framework outlined above. The judge must also have a time limit (five or ten minutes) for the questioning of each witness.

The trial starts with the prosecution briefly presenting the case, with the support of his or her witnesses, who are later cross-examined by the defence. Then the defence presents its case and witnesses (including Mr Brent) and they are then questioned by the prosecution. Finally, closing speeches are made by both sides, and the judge then sums up for the benefit of the jury, pointing out the key issues and giving guidance on points of law (for example, the accused must be proven guilty beyond reasonable doubt). The jury then reaches a decision in private (a 10-2 majority is required) and the foreman announces the verdict to the court. If the verdict is guilty, the judge then passes sentence.

Hodder & Stoughton
© 1994 Paul Higginson. The publishers grant permission for multiple copies of this sheet to be made in the place of purchase for use solely in that institution.

7 Europe

BACKGROUND TO THE EUROPEAN COMMUNITY

After the Second World War, many nations wanted to bring about peace, unity and free trade in Europe. In 1957, six countries established the European Economic Community (EEC) in order to form a larger trade market by abolishing trade barriers, in other words, a common market. So the initial motive for creating the EEC was economic. By 1986 there were twelve nations (including the UK) and the EEC had become the EC: the European Community. It was now becoming more than just an economic common market - the Single European Act (1986) aimed at closer political co-operation and the possibility of eventual political union. On 1st November 1993 all the member states had ratified the Maastricht Treaty and the EC became the European Union (EU).

EC INSTITUTIONS

1 **The European Commission** consists of 15,000 civil servants who are independent of member governments. They suggest policies to the Council of Ministers and make sure that member governments carry out EC regulations.

2 **The Council of Ministers** consists of one member from each of the twelve states. It makes EC policy, often acting on advice sent from the Commission. It shares executive authority with the Commission.

3 **The European Parliament**: each country elects a number of MEPs (Member of the European Parliament) in proportion to its total population. The principal role of the Parliament is to monitor, scrutinise and influence the work of the first two branches.

4 **The European Court of Justice** deals with problems arising from the application of EC law.

5 **Summit Conferences** are attended by leaders of member-states, who meet every six months or so to decide major policy issues.

ECONOMIC ISSUES

THE SINGLE MARKET

The Single European Act paved the way for the Single Market or '1992', which actually began on 1 January 1993. The Single Market means:

- the abolition of different regulations and barriers between EC countries, along with customs, passport checks and border controls, which lead to delays and expensive paper-work;

- the opening up of markets so that governments and large organisations can buy equipment and services from other member states, rather than just within their own country;

- an increase in investment in the EC by outside multi-national companies (particularly from the USA and Japan) which see advantages in the Single Market.

The result is that anyone can buy anything, anywhere in the EC - there are no internal barriers to trade. The European Commission has predicted that 1992 will lead to large savings for member countries and the creation of between two and five million new jobs.

Hodder & Stoughton
© 1994 Paul Higginson. The publishers grant permission for multiple copies of this sheet to be made in the place of purchase for use solely in that institution.

ECONOMIC AND MONETARY UNION

The Maastricht Treaty envisages full economic union within the EC with a European central banking system and a common currency (although Britain has the right to opt out of the final single currency). The European Monetary System (EMS) established a common currency (called the ECU) and all member countries are linked to the ECU and to each other by the Exchange Rate Mechanism (ERM). The ERM was designed to limit currency fluctuation and help align member countries' rates of inflation and interest rates. The UK was a member of the ERM but withdrew after 'Black Wednesday' in September 1992, as the pound dropped through the floor of its permitted ERM band. In 1993, as a result of immense internal pressure on certain member countries, the rules limiting currency fluctuations were relaxed, and many political commentators now feel that the ERM is effectively dead. Although Maastricht envisages a final single currency in 1999, this now seems unlikely.

❏ Questions

1 What advantages might a single currency have for a) tourists b) companies?

2 Britain has argued that a single currency will lead to the UK losing control of its economic policy to Brussels. Is this true and does it matter?

3 1992 means that you are able to study and work without restriction anywhere in Europe. What implications might this have on your future study/career plans? (Find information on opportunities for study and employment in the EC from your Careers Office.)

POLITICAL ISSUES

1 STRUCTURE

Most members of the EC are in favour of greater political (as well as economic) union. There are three possible ways for Europe to develop in the future.

Federation

Federation could mean a United States of Europe. The central government in Brussels would have control over the important areas of the economy, taxation, defence and foreign policy. Individual countries would have power over less important policies like education or local planning. The USA and Germany are examples of federations.

Confederation

Central government would have weaker powers than in a federal system. Independent national governments would be strong and play the dominant roles. Mrs Thatcher favours this idea of 'intergovernmental' decision making.

Twin-Track

A two-tier system with the ten countries moving towards a Federal Europe and the UK and Denmark (and perhaps others) opting out of the single currency and social chapter. The key question here revolves around the principle of sovereignty (complete power or authority). Should sovereignty be with a central government in Brussels or in each independent nation state?

2 NEW MEMBERS

A number of countries would like to join the EC. Austria, Finland, Norway and Sweden are set to become members in 1995 and Switzerland, Cyprus, Malta and Turkey are all eager to join an enlarged EC. Former communist states in the East like Poland, Hungary, the Czech Republic, Slovakia and the states of the old USSR will probably want to join in the future. Many would like to see a greatly expanded Europe, but could the EC cope with and manage such a large influx of new countries without damaging the interests of existing members?

Hodder & Stoughton

© 1994 Paul Higginson. The publishers grant permission for multiple copies of this sheet to be made in the place of purchase for use solely in that institution.

Former communist states would need to have an established capitalist economy and well-protected human rights before they could be admitted. New members may be reluctant to accept a common policy on defence and foreign affairs based on the North Atlantic Treaty Organisation (NATO).

❖ Discussion

1 'A Federal Europe consisting of about fifty regions might solve the troubles in Northern Ireland and recognise Scottish and Welsh nationalism, by making these areas autonomous regions within a United States of Europe.' Do you agree?

2 Are you in favour of common European armed services, or should we maintain our own army, navy and air force?

3 Is the United States of Europe a first step towards a World Government?

4 Why did John Major find it so difficult to get the Maastricht Treaty ratified by the British Parliament?

Hodder & Stoughton

© 1994 Paul Higginson. The publishers grant permission for multiple copies of this sheet to be made in the place of purchase for use solely in that institution.

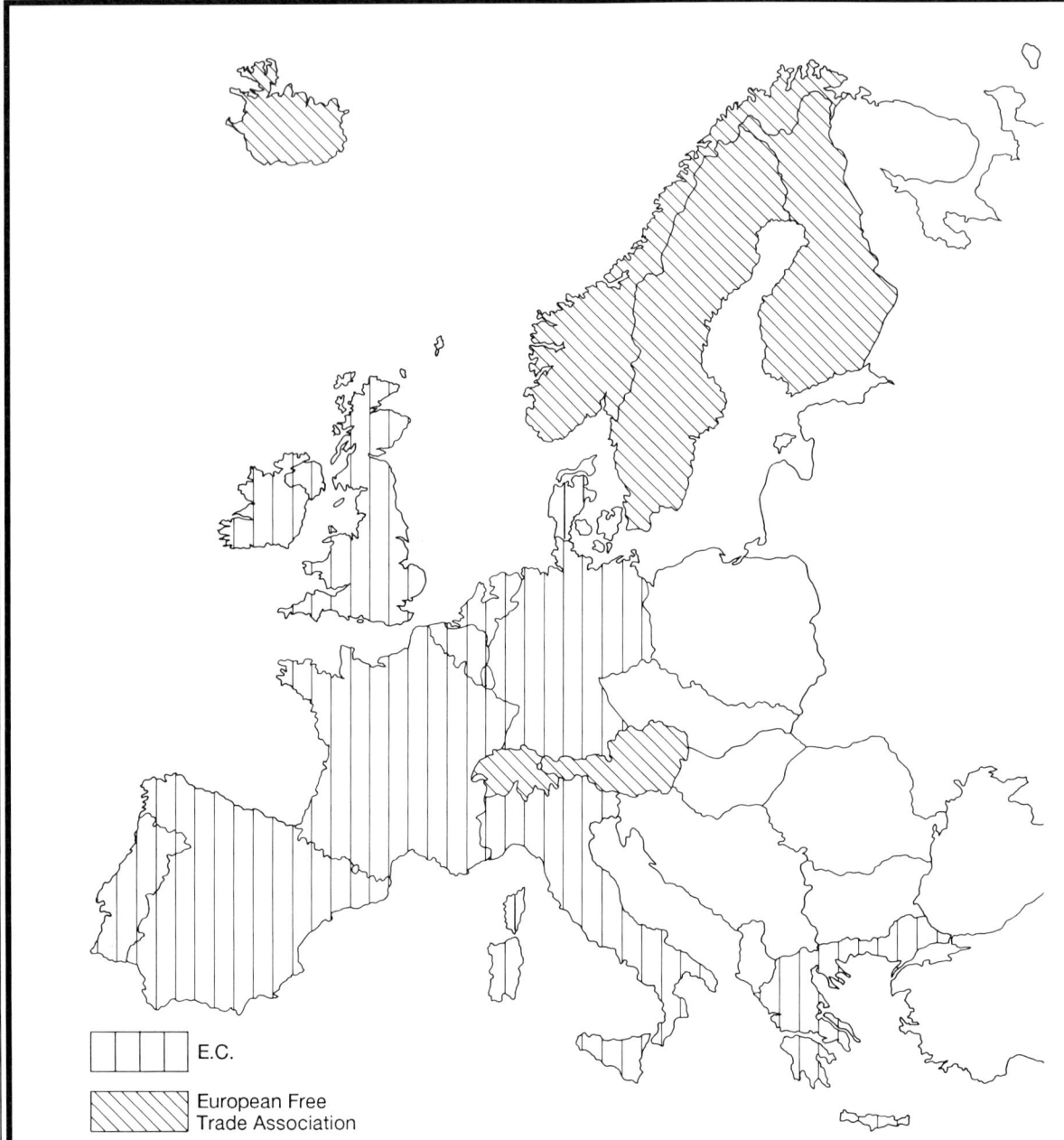

☐ E.C.

▨ European Free
Trade Association

Complete the map by writing in:

1   The twelve member states of the European Community and the six principal members of the European Free Trade Association (who agreed in 1991 to form a free-trade zone with the EC). It is assumed that the EFTA countries will eventually join the EC.

2   Write in the names of the other countries of Eastern Europe who may wish to join the EC in the future.

3   Members of the European Parliament are allocated to each country in proportion to population: one country has 99 MEPs; three have 87; one has 64; one has 31; three have 25; one has 16; one has 15; one has 6. Label the map with the correct number of MEPs.

4   These MEPs are not allocated in a totally proportional way. What unfairness exists and why?

Hodder & Stoughton

© *1994 Paul Higginson. The publishers grant permission for multiple copies of this sheet to be made in the place of purchase for use solely in that institution.*

Match the historical event with the corresponding date and then write the events out again in the correct sequence.

Greece enters the Community.	1992
West Germany, France, Italy, Belgium, Holland and Luxembourg sign the Treaty of Rome to inaugurate the EEC.	1945
The Single European Act is passed - it paves the way for an 'internal market'.	1990
The end of World War Two - there is a demand for peace and co-operation in Europe.	1957
The UK holds a referendum on continued membership of the EC. The result is a 2:1 majority in favour of staying in.	1991
The UK helps to establish the European Free Trade Association, a rival organisation to the EC.	1973
Negotiations begin to establish a European Economic Community. The UK decides not to participate.	1986
The UK, Ireland and Denmark become members of the EC.	1975
The Maastricht Treaty is signed on economic, monetary and political union.	1959
The EC becomes an internal market.	1986
Spain and Portugal bring membership up to twelve.	1956
The unification of Germany automatically brings the former East Germany and 18 million citizens into the Community.	1981

Hodder & Stoughton

© 1994 Paul Higginson. The publishers grant permission for multiple copies of this sheet to be made in the place of purchase for use solely in that institution.

Worksheet 3

SHOULD BRITAIN JOIN A UNITED STATES OF EUROPE?

What would happen if Britain joined a United States of Europe? Below are some of the arguments that have been put forward, for and against. Tick the statements you agree with.

For

Another war in Europe would be very unlikely.

It is possible to retain British culture yet be politically European.

The nation-state is finished; Europe is interdependent, and sovereignty can be 'pooled' or shared with other European countries.

Strong central government would be avoided by the principle of 'subsidiarity' (i.e. decisions are made at the lowest possible level).

The majority of business and industry agrees that there will be big increases in living standards, increased employment, greater economic prosperity, more trade.

Tough Europe-wide policies on the environment will be introduced.

A charter of basic social rights will protect citizens' rights to employment and social services.

The rest of Europe is going ahead with political union ¨ if we don't participate we will miss out on the chance to influence the future of Europe. We will be sidelined (socially, economically, and militarily).

Against

The break-up of Yugoslavia and the USSR proves that Federalism doesn't work. People want to belong to independent nation states.

British culture would be lost; we shall all become 'identikit Europeans'. Diversity is healthy.

Each country should retain sovereignty or complete authority over its own affairs.

The failure of the EC to act together during the Gulf War illustrates the need for Britain to have an independent foreign and defence policy.

Central government in Brussels would be bureaucratic, spendthrift and unaccountable.

It will be impossible for the UK to secede (withdraw) from a United States of Europe if we don't like it.

We will lose control over immigration, and large numbers of refugees or citizens from poorer countries might decide to live here.

France and Germany will dominate the new Europe and British influence will be minimal.

■ Activities

1   You may have ticked statements in both columns. Are there any contradictions in what you have ticked?

2   Organise a debate on this topic.

3   Conduct a survey of fellow students in your school or college. Ask them how much they know about Europe (federalism, 1992, single currency, Maastricht etc.) and whether they are in favour of moves towards a united Europe.

Hodder & Stoughton

© 1994 Paul Higginson. The publishers grant permission for multiple copies of this sheet to be made in the place of purchase for use solely in that institution.

8 The Media

WHAT IS THE MASS MEDIA?

The mass media are those means by which information, news and views are communicated to large, or mass, audiences. The most influential are the press and television (but other means are radio, books, pamphlets and film). It has been estimated that the average person in Britain watches about 20 hours of television per week, and approximately four hours of this is news and current affairs.

■ Activity

Conduct a survey on media use amongst your family, friends and others in the class.

1   Find out the hours spent per week: watching TV generally, watching news and current affairs programmes, reading newspapers (identify the type of paper), and listening to the radio.

2   Discover from which media source people get their daily news, and investigate how media use varies with age, sex, and social class (e.g. do those aged between 5 and 15 watch more television than any other age group?).

3   What percentage of the time do people watch television and do something else at the same time (for example, they may have the television on as background or company)?

OWNERSHIP AND CONTROL

TELEVISION

The BBC is a public company financed by television licence payments. Consequently it is obliged to serve the public interest, rather than make profits. Commercial television, on the other hand, is financed by advertising, and owned by businessmen who seek to make profits as well as serve the public interest. The Independent Television Commission (ITC) oversees, regulates and controls the 15 regional commercial television companies. There are strict controls on television to help prevent political bias and preserve impartiality - for example parties are always allocated an equitable share of air time during elections.

THE PRESS

There are no publicly-owned newspapers in Britain. Britain is unusual amongst modern democracies in having an openly biased (overwhelmingly pro-Conservative) press. Our newspapers are owned by a handful of large companies and wealthy entrepreneurs (sometimes called 'press barons'). Individuals like Rupert Murdoch own highly profitable international conglomerates which control newspapers, magazines, book publishers, commercial satellite and cable television in many different countries. Even the local press (both those on sale and free papers) is now being bought up by a few large companies - only half remains in local ownership.

IS THE MEDIA FREE?

The question of whether the media is free centres around two questions: Is the media free to report what it likes? Does the media have free access to information?

The opposing viewpoints on media freedom can be summarised under two headings - the **pluralist** view and the **dominance** view. The pluralist view states that our media are neutral, independent and free to report what they like. Because they are not controlled by the state they can be critical of the government (unlike, say, the media in China or Iraq). The dominance view says that the media reinforce, protect and advance the dominant ruling class interests of the establishment, in other words the media are an instrument of class domination.

Hodder & Stoughton © 1994 Paul Higginson. *The publishers grant permission for multiple copies of this sheet to be made in the place of purchase for use solely in that institution.*

The table below examines these two perspectives.

	Dominance View	Pluralist View
1	Most papers are openly pro-Conservative.	Most readers are unaware of the bias (a third of Sun readers believe it is a Labour paper). Television is strictly impartial.
2	The message in the media is always pro-capitalist, pro-establishment (and often racist or sexist). Not all sections of society are given equal treatment.	The media simply reflect the views of its readers or consumers. Papers must sell and television must attract viewers - the consumer gets the media he or she wants.
3	The papers and commercial television are owned and controlled by media moguls who exert great influence and control.	Editors (and their management team) control the content of papers, not the owners. Television is carefully regulated by the BBC and the ITC so that it serves the public interest.
4	Journalists generally reflect the views of their paper or station's owner. Most are middle class, university-educated, and pro-establishment. Radical journalists often have articles altered or are sacked.	Many countries in the world have media censorship. Journalists in Britain are free to say what they like as long as they don't break the law.
5	There are strict legal constraints on the media. The Official Secrets Act prevents us knowing what the government does. The libel and contempt laws, and the Obscene Publications Act further limit media freedom.	Legal constraints protect national security and individual privacy for members of the public.
6	The Government continually tries to control and use the media, for example, millions of £s are spent on privatisation campaigns, the attempt to ban Spycatcher, the ban on the broadcasting of the words of Sinn Fein leaders, the attack on Kate Adie for her 'unpatriotic' report of the US bombing of Libya, very tight control of Falklands War broadcasting.	The Government does not censor or control the media. If the media always served the ruling dominant class or establishment why would governments try so hard to manipulate them? Politicians often fail to control the media (for example, the showing of 'Death on the Rock'). Some programmes often pressure the government into action (for example, Rough Justice and the Guildford Four).
7	Only the rich can own a newspaper or television station, or take legal action in the courts.	In a free society anyone can set up a newspaper.

❖ Discussion

1 Does the Sun print page three women because people want them in the paper (i.e. is it meeting a consumer need?), or did it create the need in the first place? Do newspapers create needs or simply respond to them?

2 Some politicians would like to see a state-owned newspaper, i.e. one owned by the public, rather than an individual or company. What is your view?

3 It has been suggested that the government should scrap the BBC licence fee and allow it to accept advertising. What would be the pros and cons of such a reform?

Hodder & Stoughton

© 1994 Paul Higginson. The publishers grant permission for multiple copies of this sheet to be made in the place of purchase for use solely in that institution.

4 The tabloid newspapers often pry into the private lives of celebrities and those in the public eye. Is this press freedom or an abuse of an individual's privacy?

5 Why has the government banned the broadcasting of the speech of Sinn Fein leaders? Is this an unnecessary constraint on media freedom?

6 During times of war (especially World War Two) and crisis the government and the media often create disinformation by dishonest reporting. Should the media always report the truth, come what may?

■ Activities - Newspaper Headlines

1 We have seen that there are ways of classifying newspapers, for example, popular versus quality, pro-Conservative versus pro-Labour. The reports you read may describe the same event in very different ways according to the type of newspaper. Get hold of two opposing types of paper published on the same day and compare their treatment of the same news events. Watch out for bias, and try to distinguish between the facts of the case and the opinions of the writer.

2 The election in April 1992 produced the following results (1987 figures in brackets)

Conservative 336 (375); Labour 271 (229); Liberal Democrats 20 (22); Others 24 (24)

Below are two different interpretations of the result, one pro-Conservative, the other pro-Labour:

Major's Triumph

'Last night John Major confounded all the opinion pollsters and political pundits by romping home to gain a clear overall majority of 22 seats over all the other parties. This quite clearly shows not only his massive personal popularity but the trust the British people place in Conservative policies and ideas'.

Labour Gain 42 Seats

'The Tories were down by 39 seats from their 1987 total yesterday, as Labour increased its MPs from 229 in 1987 to 271. After a brilliant campaign Neil Kinnock brought Labour to within a whisker of victory and the increase in Labour MPs is a testimony to the policy changes he has engineered in recent years. A vicious personal campaign against Kinnock in the media was the major factor preventing an overall Labour win.'

Write similar short headlines and articles giving two different perspectives from two different papers - either popular and quality or Labour and Conservative on the following events:

1 A police chief says there has been a big increase in crimes committed by young blacks.
2 Arthur Scargill, the miners' leader, presses for strike action to 'try to prevent pit closure and job losses'.
3 Lambeth Council gives a grant to a local Womens Group.
4 The Royal Family is to get an increase in its Civil List payment above the rate of inflation.
5 A Conservative Cabinet Minister enters hospital for private hip replacement.
6 French farmers stop trucks containing British lambs from entering the country, claiming they are putting them out of business.

3 Newswatch - Watch the news tonight on both ITV and BBC (try watching the Nine o'clock News on BBC One, then the News at Ten on ITV). Write down the running order of the stories and time the length of each item, e.g. BBC: PMs speech 5 mins, N. Ireland bomb 4 mins, US election 3 mins, etc., ITV: US election 6 mins, PMs speech 4 mins, Famine in Africa 3 mins.

Compare the way the same events are portrayed on different channels, or given greater or lesser importance. Were there any events that were not regarded as newsworthy at all on one channel but given prominence on the other? Examine how far the bulletins were centred on this country and on British people (e.g. 'Huge death toll in Russian plane crash - no Britons killed').

Hodder & Stoughton   © 1994 Paul Higginson. The publishers grant permission for multiple copies of this sheet to be made in the place of purchase for use solely in that institution.

Worksheet 1
The British Press

Owner	Title	Average Daily Sale (000s)	Sunday/ Daily	Type Popular/ Quality	Political Affiliation
News International (owned by Rupert Murdoch)	News of the World	4,768			
	Sun	3,571			
	Sunday Times	1,167			
	Today	533			
	Times	386			
Mirror Group Newspapers plc	Mirror	2,903			
	Sunday Mirror	2,774			
	Sunday People	2,165			
United Newspapers	Express	1,526			
	Sunday Express	1,666			
	Star	806			
Guardian Newspapers	Guardian	541			
	Observer	429			
Pearson	Financial Times	290			
Daily Mail & General Trust	Mail	1,675			
	Mail on Sunday	1,941			
Hollinger	Daily Telegraph	1,038			
	Sunday Telegraph	558			
Newspaper Publishing	Independent	300			
	Independent on Sunday	320			

1 In the columns provided, write in whether the paper is a Sunday or a daily, the political affiliation of each paper (i.e. which party it supported at the last election) and the type (papers are usually classified into popular/quality, or tabloid/broadsheet).

2 Calculate the percentage of newspapers that are controlled by the Big Three (News International, Mirror Group Newspapers, and United Newspapers). Do this for both the Sunday and daily circulation, basing your calculation on the number of copies sold.

3 Calculate the percentage of newspapers (in terms of copies sold) that support the Conservative Party. Does it matter that this is so high?

4 What percentage of total copy sales are quality papers?

5 Total newspaper sales dropped by 626,000 from 1991 to 1992. Suggest reasons for this.

Hodder & Stoughton

© 1994 Paul Higginson. The publishers grant permission for multiple copies of this sheet to be made in the place of purchase for use solely in that institution.

The media, and especially television, play a very important part in people's lives. But exactly how much influence do the media have on us, and in what ways does it influence and effect society? Examine the statements below, ticking the appropriate box, and then compare your answers in groups of three.

	Strongly agree	Agree	Disagree	Strongly disagree
1 Violence on television causes people to behave more violently.				
2 Media advertising persuades and often cons people into buying products they often don't really want or need.				
3 The media bring an enormous amount of pleasure to vast numbers of people.				
4 Television makes people conform to certain values or ideas - it brainwashes people into believing in certain things, such as materialism, or capitalism.				
5 Because of commercial advertising and the need to make profits, the standard and quality of programmes is lower on ITV than BBC.				
6 Television numbs the brain and stops people from questioning and thinking for themselves - it is 'chewing gum for the eyes'.				
7 Television has contributed to a decline in moral standards.				
8 Television is a friend for the lonely, elderly or infirm. It helps people to pass the time.				
9 Since the advent of television, families talk to each other less, and time spent pursuing creative hobbies or activities has decreased.				
10 Soap operas are addictive fantasy. Many people are more concerned about fictional events in Coronation Street than the reality of famine in Ethiopa.				
11 The media, especially the tabloid press, help to reinforce racist and sexist stereotypes.				
12 Television has contributed to a heightened awareness of current affairs and important issues through education and news programmes.				
13 Freedom of choice means that if you don't like what you see on television you can switch it off. People - not governments - should censor.				
14 It is wrong for the media to place more emphasis on the Royal Family than on issues like world hunger or the environment.				
15 It is wrong for Spitting Image to assert that everyone in the public eye is fair game for ridicule.				
16 Neil Kinnock was right to say that the media campaign against Labour was a major reason for its defeat in the 1992 General Election.				

Hodder & Stoughton

© 1994 Paul Higginson. The publishers grant permission for multiple copies of this sheet to be made in the place of purchase for use solely in that institution.

The Television News

Get into groups of five. This simulation involves you in writing and presenting a four minute national news bulletin.

The stories below have arrived on the newsdesk during the day. Select the most important (you will have to leave out some stories), and prioritise them.

Elaborate on the items, include quotes, statistics and additional information and write the script for each item.

Decide on the format you will use - one newsreader, or two alternating. You will then have exactly four minutes to read out your bulletin - this must be *exactly* four minutes so you will need someone to count the newsreader in and out.

1   Leader of the Opposition says that standards in British schools are falling.

2   Crime figures for UK show another big increase - especially for violent crime.

3   Five killed in pile up on M25.

4   IRA bomb explodes in Belfast - no injuries

5   Rod Stewart wins record libel damages over article in Sunday World newspaper.

6   Ethiopia in the grip of famine - millions at risk of starvation says UN.

7   England manager announces team for big international against Germany.

8   Hole in ozone layer is getting bigger, claims top Oxford scientist.

9   Man arrested after policeman is killed during armed robbery in London.

10 Ching-Ching, London Zoo's popular panda gives birth to twins.

11 Member of royal family fined £100 for speeding.

12 Cabinet re-shuffle - new Minister for Trade and Industry.

Hodder & Stoughton

© 1994 Paul Higginson. *The publishers grant permission for multiple copies of this sheet to be made in the place of purchase for use solely in that institution.*

9 Poverty

What is Poverty?

There are two types of poverty - absolute and relative. Seebohm Rowntree defined absolute poverty as insufficient income "for the maintenance of merely physical efficiency". Essentially this means a lack of food, clothing and shelter. Many people in the Third World suffer from absolute poverty: 15 million children die each year through lack of food and clean water. Few in Britain can be classified as absolutely poor, but many people live in poverty compared to (relative to) the living standard of the average citizen. This relative poverty applies to those who have such a low income that they are unable to have what is considered a normal lifestyle.

There are several ways of determining what constitutes relative poverty in Britain.

- those on or below the minimum level of income provided by the government in the form of social security - this is sometimes termed the 'poverty line'. Approximately 6.2 million people come into this category;
- those able to survive but unable to acquire what the rest of society considers as necessities (calculated at 7.5 million people.);
- those with an income below half the national average (7.7 million people);
- those living in a deprived or impoverished environment compared to others in society, for example, those suffering from poor housing and public services, inner-city pollution, a high crime rate, etc..

In 1983, MORI conducted surveys of what people regarded as necessary for a basic standard of life and what they could and could not afford. Out of a population of 56 million, 6 million people were unable to afford adequate clothing, 3.5 million could not afford carpets, a fridge or a washing machine, and over 3 million had inadequate heating. From this it was estimated that 13 per cent of the population was in relative poverty in the 1980s.

Groups Affected by Poverty

Using the measure of 'less than half of the average income' it is possible to identify five major groups affected by relative poverty in Britain.

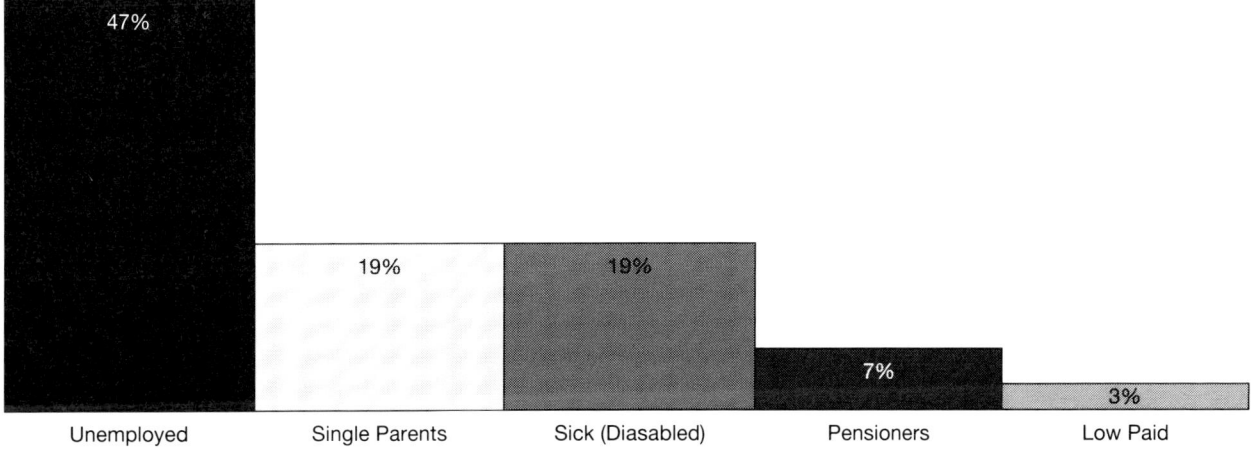

People suffering from relative poverty in the UK (1992)

The percentage figures in the graph show the number of people with incomes below half the average, for example 47 per cent of all unemployed people come into this category.

Hodder & Stoughton   © 1994 Paul Higginson. The publishers grant permission for multiple copies of this sheet to be made in the place of purchase for use solely in that institution.

The next figure gives the total number of people who were described as relatively poor in 1985 and 1987. What explanations might there be for these figures?

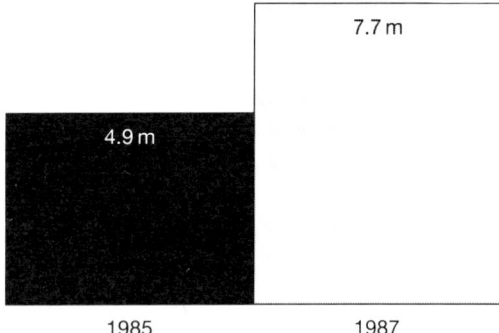

Total number of people classed as relatively poor in 1985 and 1987

❏ Questions

1   Find out the current rate of unemployment. Is it rising or falling? What kind of jobs have been in decline in recent years?

2   One in seven families in Britain is now a single parent family. What problems might such families have in terms of maintaining an adequate income?

3   Between 1981 and 87 average income rose by 20 per cent, but for the low-paid the rise was just 2 per cent. What kind of jobs are low-paid and why do women workers make up the majority in this category?

4   Living standards for most pensioners have increased in recent years. Suggest reasons for this.

Some of the Main Social Security Benefits

• Retirement pensions are paid to all women at 60, and to men at 65.
• Income support is Means tested (it replaced supplementary benefit).
• Child benefit is paid to all children (more for the first child) regardless of family's income. - Family credit is paid to the low-paid as a top up.
• The Social Fund provides grants and more often loans for those with special needs.
• Housing, Invalidity, Unemployment, and Sickness benefits. For those in particular circumstances.

RICH AND POOR

There is a huge gap between the rich and the poor in Britain. Study these tables which show the distribution of income and wealth (Social Trends 1992).

Wealth		
(property, shares, savings etc.)		
% of the population	% of national wealth owned	
	1976	1989
Top 1%	21%	18%
Top 10%	50%	53%
Top 50%	92%	94%
Bottom 50%	8%	6%

Income after Tax		
% of the population	% of national income received	
	1977	1988
Top 20%	43%	50%
Next 20%	26%	25%
Middle 20%	18%	16%
Next 20%	10%	7%
Bottom 20%	3%	2%

Hodder & Stoughton   © 1994 Paul Higginson. The publishers grant permission for multiple copies of this sheet to be made in the place of purchase for use solely in that institution.

There is also a marked North/South divide. The table below shows the regional differences in personal income (with 100% as the UK average):

Regional Income Differences

South East	114%	Midlands	91%
South West	105%	North of England	91%
East Anglia	100%	Wales	88%
Scotland	96%	Northern Ireland	87%

Life Expencancy at Birth

	Women	Men
Ireland	77	71
Britain	79	73
Germany	79	73
Canada	81	75
Japan	82	76

Poor health and poverty are linked. Major illness like heart disease and cancer are more prevalent in the poorer sections of society, and the death rate is higher compared to more affluent social classes. Moreover, life expectancy in British pensioners is much worse than in other comparable countries.

❑ Questions

1 Has the gap between rich and poor increased in recent years?

2 Why is so much wealth held in so few hands? Is this situation morally acceptable?

3 What are the pros and cons of large scale wealth re-distribution?

4 'A teacher in rural Wales is much better off than one in the South East'. In what ways might this be true and how might the statistics in the table of regional income differences be deceptive?

5 In what ways might the North/South divide increase in the 1990s (think about 1992, the Channel Tunnel, etc.)

6 Suggest reasons why British pensioners do not live as long as those in some other countries.

❖ Discussion

Debate this motion: This House believes 'the poor are always with us'.

■ Activity: Case-study

You are 70 years old, unmarried, living in rented accommodation (Imagine a one-bedroom flat). You are a typical low-income pensioner with no savings, no occupational pension from your former hairdressing job and no other source of income.

Your weekly income (using 1993-94 figures) comprises: State Retirement Pension £56.10 (you have paid all your national insurance contributions and so receive the full pension) plus £5.20 Income Support top up. Your total income is therefore £61.30 per week.

As you are on Income Support your rent is paid in full, you receive a full rebate on your council tax, and dental treatment and eye tests are free. However, you will have to pay other weekly outgoings. These are gas and electricity £7.63, water £1.40, television licence (colour) £1.53. (These are average figures taken from recent surveys.)

Calculate what you need to spend on food, drink and household goods (soap, washing-up liquid, etc.) Ask your parents, grandparents or neighbours if you are unsure of prices. Then divide the rest between clothes, shoes, newspapers, bus fares, presents for relatives, entertainment, outings and anything else you feel you might need.

At present you don't possess a telephone - can you afford one? What would you do if you needed to repair or replace a major item (e.g. a washing machine)? Are you able to save any money for a rainy day? Discuss the implications of your findings in the group.

Hodder & Stoughton

© 1994 Paul Higginson. The publishers grant permission for multiple copies of this sheet to be made in the place of purchase for use solely in that institution.

Worksheet 1
Necessities or Luxuries?

One way of determining relative poverty in the 1990s is to classify what items and activities people feel are important in order to have a reasonable standard of life. Go through the list below and identify what you consider are necessities (N) and luxuries (L). Then rank them in order of importance 1 to 24, with 1 as the most necessary. Remember we are talking about what is necessary for a decent standard of living, not for survival.

	N / L	Rank		N / L	Rank
Annual holiday			Safe place for children to play		
Car			Microwave oven		
Washing machine			Roast joint once a week		
Adequate heating for main rooms			New trainers for children		
Toys for young children			Public park in easy walking distance		
New clothes (not second hand)			Television		
Crime-free neighbourhood			Buying birthday and Christmas presents		
Meat or fish every day			Video recorder		
Winter coat			Local hospital with no or very small waiting lists		
Adequate efficient public transport			Two pints of beer (or equivalent) per week		
Ten cigarettes per day			Garden		
Telephone					
Evening out once a week					

✪ Further study

1 Compare the replies of all the group. If 50 per cent or more of the group say an item is a necessity, class it as such, if less, then class it as a luxury. How many items and activities has your group labelled as necessities?

2 Draw up a group ranking based on the number of people saying an item is a necessity. Compare this group ranking with your individual ranking.

3 In a survey conducted in 1983 only 51 per cent of people said that a TV was a necessity. Do you think this figure would be different today? (What was the figure for your class?) What might this suggest about the poverty line?

4 Ask your parents or grandparents to say if they had the above items when they were your age. If they didn't, does it mean they were poor?

Hodder & Stoughton

© 1994 Paul Higginson. The publishers grant permission for multiple copies of this sheet to be made in the place of purchase for use solely in that institution.

What Causes Poverty?

There are many different theories used to explain the existence of poverty in Britain. In groups of three, examine the ideas below and rank them in order of importance beginning with the factory you feel best explains the existence of poverty.

1   Poverty is passed on from one generation to the next through the process of socialisation (a cycle of deprivation). The poor live in poor neighbourhoods, receive a poor education and a poor job and produce poor children.

2   The poor have certain values, beliefs and habits such as resignation to their lot, feelings of worthlessness and inferiority, lack of planning for future, a general feeling of helplessness, and poor motivation.

3   The poor lack power to change their situation; they do not join pressure groups, political parties or trade unions. Many don't vote or participate in the decision making process so they are ignored by politicians.

4   Many don't claim all the benefits which are available through the welfare state.

5   The poor are lazy - they become dependent on social security so there is no incentive to work.

6   As social and economic changes occur many suffer through no fault of their own. For example, increased technology has led to higher levels of unemployment.

7   Lack of intelligence or ability means the poor are unemployed or low-paid.

8   The capitalist system accepts (and perhaps needs) a certain amount of poverty: a large number of unemployed people reduces strikes and encourages those in work to accept low wages, thereby increasing profits for big business. Free-market politicians will always look after the interests of the better off (by giving tax cuts) rather than the poor.

9   The benefit system does not provide adequate payments to groups like pensioners, single parents, etc.

When you have discerned the causes of poverty you can better decide how and if poverty can be eliminated. Draw up a list of practical suggestions for helping to reduce poverty.

Hodder & Stoughton   © 1994 Paul Higginson. *The publishers grant permission for multiple copies of this sheet to be made in the place of purchase for use solely in that institution.*

Worksheet 3
The Welfare State

The Welfare State was established by the Labour Government of 1945-50 to combat 'want, disease, ignorance, squalor and idleness' (Beveridge Report). Free education, the NHS and a comprehensive benefits system were introduced. However, in the 1980s and 1990s many assumptions behind welfare policy have been debated.

What is your view on the following questions? Think of arguments for and against each idea.

1 Should those with money be encouraged to purchase private health care, education, and pension schemes?

2 If people do buy their services privately should they continue to have to support the public services through high taxation?

3 Should benefits be universal (given to all), like child benefit, or should they be selective, i.e. targeted on those who really need them (e.g. The Social Fund).

4 Should able-bodied unemployed people have their benefit stopped if they refuse jobs that are offered to them?

5 How far should people be expected to move about the country ('get on their bikes') in order to find work?

6 Should benefits be means-tested? i.e. should those applying for benefit have to prove their low income or wealth by providing detailed information on savings, bank accounts, etc.

7 Should doctors' prescriptions be free for all or only for those on a low income or benefit (as at present)?

8 Should private companies be allowed to run welfare services (like old people's homes)?

9 Should people who stay at home to look after old, sick, or disabled relatives receive a 'carer's wage' from the government?

10 Should a minimum wage be introduced?

11 Should unemployed under-18 year olds who leave home have their benefit stopped?

12 Should men and women both receive a retirement pension at the age of 63? (At present men receive their pension at 65, women at 60.)

13 Should we rely more on efficient voluntary agencies (like the Salvation Army) rather than the state to care for the poor?

14 Should taxes on the very rich be increased in order to raise benefits for the poor?

15 In parts of the US, the unemployed must spend a part of each day working for their benefit, (picking up litter, street cleaning, etc.). if they refuse to do this their benefit is stopped. Should this 'Workfare' scheme be introduced here?

Hodder & Stoughton   © 1994 Paul Higginson. The publishers grant permission for multiple copies of this sheet to be made in the place of purchase for use solely in that institution.

10 Gender

The physical and biological differences between men and women are referred to as sex differences. The different roles and patterns of behaviour men and women are expected to perform are described as gender differences. These roles are often passed on to us through the process of socialisation: our upbringing, family and friends, the media, education, religion, etc.

SEXISM

Discrimination against one sex (regarding that sex as inferior to the other) is referred to as sexism. Although women are usually the victims of sexist attitudes and treatment, the term can also be used to describe the unfair treatment of men.

■ Activity

List six examples of sexist attitudes or behaviour (three against women, three against men). What are the consequences of sexism, and in what ways can it be eliminated from our society?

NATURE V NURTURE

Study the following extracts:

"Men and women are biologically different, they have different physical attributes. A woman is able to bear a child and breastfeed for example, so it is only natural for her to take the dominant role in child-rearing. Men are physically able to do more manual jobs, so it is not surprising that most labourers on building sites are men. Because men and women are biologically different it is inconceivable that the top woman weight-lifter or sprinter will ever beat the top man. Most of the differences between the sexes are a result of nature not socialisation. Even very small boys brought up in a non-sexist way will be naturally more aggressive and physically stronger than girls."

"From the point of birth onwards we are socialised and nurtured in ways that prepare us for our roles in later life. Society provides us with our values, beliefs and characteristics, as well as role-models for us to copy. Women have proved that there is no biological reason why they can't be Prime Ministers, doctors, judges, bus drivers or engineers. Similarly, men have shown that they are quite able to become midwives, home economics teachers or bring up children at home. If we socialise our children in non-sexist ways then the differences between men and women in later life will disappear".

■ Activities

1 Debate
   Debate 'Nature v Nurture?' using the arguments above, either in the group, or better still in the whole school.

2 Household Jobs Survey
   How do men and women divide up tasks around the house? Interview some couples (preferably both working full time) and find out who does what. Ask who generally:
   • cooks the meals;
   • does the shopping;
   • washes and irons the clothes;
   • does the garden;
   • repairs the car and household appliances;
   • cleans the toilet;
   • washes the dishes;
   • dusts and cleans the house.
   Share your findings with the class.

Hodder & Stoughton   © 1994 Paul Higginson. The publishers grant permission for multiple copies of this sheet to be made in the place of purchase for use solely in that institution.

THE MEDIA

Newspapers and television often reinforce stereotypes by the use of sexist language and pictures.

■ Activities

1   Watch the adverts on television tonight and note down the different roles depicted by men and women. Pay particular attention to adverts for washing powder, washing-up liquid, food, cars, lager, chocolates and D.I.Y. goods. How do the adverts for after-shave and perfume portray people (especially women) as sex-objects?

2   Cut out three adverts from magazines for newspapers which use sexist language or pictures and bring them into class for discussion.

EDUCATION

Should girls and boys be educated separately or together? Many educationalists argue that single-sex schools are better for girls. Study the arguments below.

Together	Separate
1 Promotes understanding and tolerance.	1 Exam results seem to indicate that girls do better when taught separately (especially in science subjects).
2 Prepares young people for adult life, e.g. workplace or university.	2 In mixed classrooms girls receive less attention than boys. Moreover boys tend to take most of the positions of responsibility in a mixed school.
3 It is natural and leads to a healthy social development; single-sex schools often lead to difficulties integrating later on.	3 Girls become more self-confident and assertive when taught separately.
4 Boosts self confidence and feelings of togetherness, not just socially but academically and in areas of sport and hobbies.	4 Girls don't suffer socially - they still see and meet boys outside school.

❑ Questions

1   Which type of school did you attend - co-educational or single-sex? Which of the above arguments seem to fit in with your experience?

2   In a recent survey, parents said they wanted co-education for their sons but single sex for their daughters. Why is this?

Hodder & Stoughton

© 1994 Paul Higginson. The publishers grant permission for multiple copies of this sheet to be made in the place of purchase for use solely in that institution.

■ Activities

1 Classroom Survey

Studies have shown that in mixed classes boys receive more attention from teachers than girls. Conduct your own survey! Note down the number of:

a. questions the teacher asks boys/girls (does the sex of the teacher make a difference here?);

b. answers volunteered by boys/girls;

c. contributions to class discussion (does one sex dominate?);

d. times (if any) when the lesson is disrupted by boys/girls.

You should then be able to quantify in percentage terms the involvement of boys and girls in particular lessons.

2 Subject Choice

Many more boys than girls choose science, maths, technology and computing subjects at school and college. Girls heavily outnumber boys in subjects like art, languages, religious education and home economics. See if this is true in your group. Below are a number of reasons why this might be - list these points in order of importance from 1 to 6, and then compare your views with others in the group.

1 Boys are naturally better at sciences and maths than girls.

2 Girls and boys have traditionally always done certain subjects.

3 Teachers guide or advise students to go in certain directions.

4 Pressure from parents and peers.

5 Subject choice is determined by future career plans.

6 Boys are more confident and assertive in science; girls feel threatened in mixed classes in certain subjects.

EQUALITY AND THE LAW

Parliament passed five important Acts in the 1970s and 1980s to help prevent discrimination.

- **The Equal Pay Act** (1970) stated that men and women doing the same job should be paid at the same rate. The Act was amended in 1985 to enable equal pay for work of 'equal value' (defined in relation to effort, skill, responsibility, etc.).

- **The Employment Protection Act** (1975) allows a woman the right to paid maternity leave and the right to return to her previous employer after the child is born.

- **The Sex Discrimination Act** (1975) makes it unlawful to discriminate against anyone because of their sex.

- **The Equal Opportunities Commission** (1975) was set up to oversee these Acts.

- **The Employment Act** (1989) swept away most restrictions on the employment of women (e.g. in mines).

Hodder & Stoughton   © 1994 Paul Higginson. The publishers grant permission for multiple copies of this sheet to be made in the place of purchase for use solely in that institution.

❑ Questions

1 Despite the Equal Pay Act, women's average wages are still only three-quarters that of men's. Why is this?

2 What problems arise from trying to decide what is 'equal value' (for example, between a female midwife and a male electrician)?

3 Why was the Employment Protection Act so important for many women?

4 Think of three examples of sex discrimination which would be illegal under the sex Discrimination Act (in employment, education and housing).

5 The armed forces are exempt from the Sex Discrimination Act (for example, British women are not permitted to carry weapons and fight in the front-line). Should this be changed, as in the US and Israeli armies?

6 The Equal Opportunities Commission has reported that despite these Acts much discrimination still exists. Suggest reasons for this.

■ Activities

What Happened When?

Below are a number of key events in the movement towards greater sexual equality. Put them in historical order with the appropriate date.

---

1 Women over 21 years old given vote - equality with men achieved.

2 Women conscripted to armed forces.

3 Church of England votes to ordain women.

4 The Women's Liberation Movement holds first demonstration at the 'Miss World' contest.

5 First suffragettes are imprisoned.

6 Nancy Astor becomes the first woman MP.

7 Margaret Thatcher becomes the first woman Prime Minister in Britain.

8 Women over 30 years old get the vote.

9 House of Lords open its doors to women.

1905 1918 1919 1928 1941 1958 1969 1979 1992

Hodder & Stoughton   © 1994 Paul Higginson. The publishers grant permission for multiple copies of this sheet to be made in the place of purchase for use solely in that institution.

WOMEN IN POLITICS

Study the graph below.

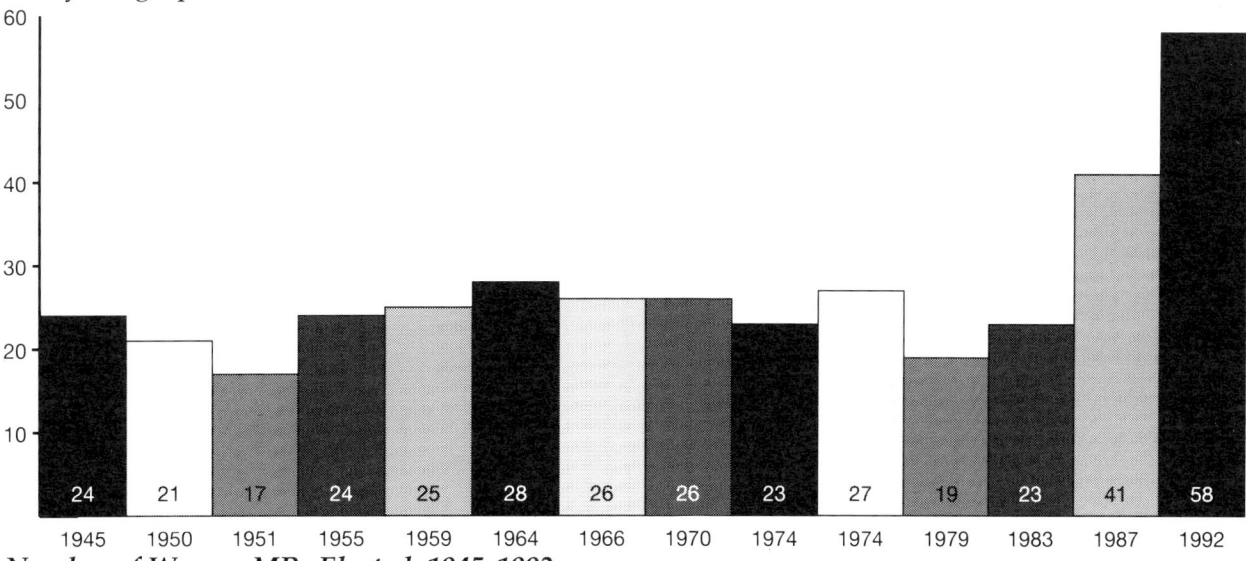

Number of Women MPs Elected, 1945-1992

❑ Questions

1   Suggest reasons why there are so few women MPs.

2   Male Labour and Conservative candidates standing in 1992 were twice as likely to win their seats as female candidates. Suggest two possible reasons for this.

3   In Scandinavia some political parties have ruled that 50 per cent of all candidates for office must be women. What are the advantages and disadvantages of adopting such a policy?

4   What other reforms would you suggest to increase the number of women in Parliament?

5   Politics is not just about Parliament. List other areas in which women have been politically active, for example, Greenham Common, and Women Against the Pit Closures.

HOW DO YOU SPEND YOUR TIME?

Each member of the class keeps a record for a week of how many hours he or she devotes to various tasks. Divide the week into four categories: sleep, academic work, leisure, household jobs (e.g. shopping, preparing meals, washing up, supervising younger children, etc.). If the class is single sex ask another student of the same age (but opposite sex) to do the survey in his or her class. You should have approximately the same number of male and female participants in the survey. Compare results and see if there are significant male/female differences.

VISITING SPEAKERS

Invite one or more working women to come and talk to the group about employment opportunities, sexism in the workplace and equal opportunities.

Hodder & Stoughton

© 1994 Paul Higginson. The publishers grant permission for multiple copies of this sheet to be made in the place of purchase for use solely in that institution.

Worksheet 1
Socialisation

Complete the boxes below with the stereotypical male/female differences.

		MALE	FEMALE
1	The colour of a baby's room	Blue	
2	Typical toys		Dolls
3	Types of children's clothes		
4	Adult response to a child falling over		Hugs and cuddles
5	Playground games		
6	Sports		
7	Comics/reading material		
8	Games adults play with a child		
9	Attitude of adults to a child getting dirty		
10	Attitude of adults to a child making lots of noise	Outgoing, boisterous, lively, enthusiastic	Emotional, 'unladylike', highly-strung
11	Subjects studied at school		
12	Attitude of adults to a child crying		
13	Attitude of adults to a child carrying heavy objects		
14	Attitude of adults to an older child hugging Mummy		
15	Attitude of adults to a child getting into fights		

Make a list of all the traditional male/female qualities. Discuss your findings in the group. How important is childhood socialisation in shaping adult gender roles?

❖ Discussion

1 Were you socialised in a stereotypical way?

2 What difficulties might parents encounter if they try to bring children up in a non-sexist way?

3 Compare your socialisation with that of your parents or grandparents. In what ways have things changed?

4 Examine your list of male/female qualities. What consequences might these qualities have for the careers mean and women follow?

Hodder & Stoughton

© 1994 Paul Higginson. The publishers grant permission for multiple copies of this sheet to be made in the place of purchase for use solely in that institution.

Worksheet 2

Women and Work

Circle the correct answers.

1 The average women's wage in Britain is

   (a) the same as men's wage   (b) 85% of men's wage   (c) 75% of men's wage.

2 What proportion of judges and university professors are women?

   (a) 1%   (b) 10%   (c) 25%

3 How much of the UK workforce is female?

   (a) 12%   (b) 28%   (c) 43%

4 How many single parent families are there in Britain (most are headed by a woman)?

   (a) 500,000   (b) 750,000   (c) 1 million

5 If a housewife were to get paid for her work, her estimated weekly earnings would be

   (a) £140   (b) £280   (c) £420.

6 In families where both partners are in paid employment the woman does more work around the house than the man. How many more hours per week?

   (a) 6 hours   (b) 11 hours   (c) 16 hours

7 How much of the world's work is done by women?

   (a) one third   (b) a half   (c) two thirds

8 How much of the world's income do women receive?

   (a) 10%   (b) 30%   (c) 50%

9 How much of the world's property do women own?

   (a) 20%   (b) 10%   (c) 1%

10 In Africa, how much of the planting, harvesting, weeding, and livestock care is undertaken by women?

   (a) 50%   (b) 70%   (c) 90%

11 In India how many women workers are there in the building industry?

   (a) 25%   (b) 50%   (c) 75%

12 In many countries girls miss out on education because they have to say at home and do domestic work. How many of the world's illiterate are female?

   (a) 50%   (b) 60%   (c) 70%

● **Group work**

Try to think of explanations for some of these statistics. Why does such a situation exist and what can be done to change it?

Hodder & Stoughton   © 1994 Paul Higginson. The publishers grant permission for multiple copies of this sheet to be made in the place of purchase for use solely in that institution.

Worksheet 3
The Ordination of Women

There has been a great deal of debate recently on the issue of women in the priesthood; in 1992 the General Synod of the Church of England voted for the first time in its history to ordain women, and the first ordinations took place in 1994.

The boxes below contain a number of arguments used to suggest that women should be ordained. Think of counter-arguments (giving reasons and examples) and complete the appropriate boxes.

Women Priests in the Church of England

Argument	Counter-Argument
1 Jesus was both God and Man, therefore a priest should also be a man.	
2 All Jesus' 12 disciples were men.	
3 Jesus had many radical new ideas but makes no mention of women priests in the Gospels.	
4 There have never been women priests in 2,000 years of Church history and tradition.	
5 A large minority of the Church is opposed to women priests (and many have said they will leave if women are ordained). Their views and feelings should be respected.	
6 The Roman Catholic Church is opposed to the ordination of women - this could be a serious setback to ecumenism (Christian unity).	
7 Women would not command the same respect and authority in the pulpit as men.	
8 God created men and women differently, to do different things. Women are not inferior to men, they are just called upon to fulfil different roles in the Church.	
9 If women priests had children they would not be able to devote enough time to their parishioners.	
10 If in doubt the best course of action is to leave things as they are.	
11 During Communion the priest takes on the role of Jesus Christ at the Last Supper. How can a woman do this?	
12 It will cause a schism - or split - in the Church. Many male clergy will refuse to accept women priests.	

✿ Further study

Discuss your ideas in the group. Find out the views of other denominations and non-Christian faiths on the subject of women and religion.

Hodder & Stoughton

© 1994 Paul Higginson. The publishers grant permission for multiple copies of this sheet to be made in the place of purchase for use solely in that institution.

11 Race and Ethnic Minorities

Although there are three main races, Negro, Mongoloid and Caucasian, intermixing has created a large number of sub-groups. Although some people (like the Nazis in Germany) have argued that racial groups have distinct personality traits or characteristics, this is inaccurate and can lead to racism - discrimination based on the idea that one race is superior to another.

Ethnic groups are those which have a common historical, social and cultural background. In Britain the ethnic majority is white, and there are many ethnic minorities.

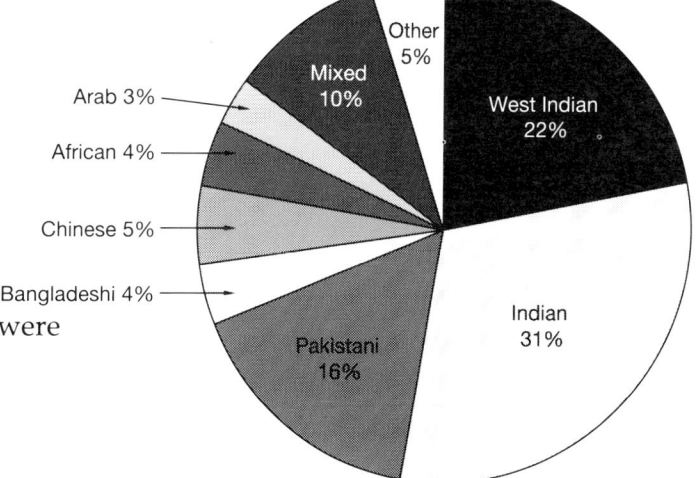

Ethnic minorities in the UK.

The pie chart represents approximately 3m people, i.e. around 5.5 per cent of the total population of Britain. Of these, 43 per cent were born in Britain.

WHAT CAUSES RACISM?

Racism, the belief that one racial group is inferior to others, can be caused by many factors.

1   Scapegoating. Minorities are often blamed for social problems (for example, a lack of jobs or housing, or a high crime rate). Frustration and anger are often directed at weaker sections of society, who are least able to retaliate.

2   Racism promotes integration and unity amongst the majority. Some governments have increased their own power by whipping up racism against 'outsiders'.

3   Stereotyping. This is the view that minority groups have shared 'different' characteristics which are seen as inferior or a threat to the majority.

4   Fear based on misunderstandings and a lack of knowledge of the minority culture.

5   Economic envy can develop when minorities are perceived as doing better than members of the majority group.

6   History. Colonialism and the slave trade established the idea of a superior Western culture civilising inferior black people.

7   Media influence. Some tabloid newspapers have reinforced racial stereotypes, especially with regard to black crime rates.

8   Anxiety about 'swamping'. This is the fear, often fanned by right wing parties like the National Front, that one ethnic group or another is taking over. Many majority group members feel they will lose their traditional identity and culture in a multi-cultural Britain.

9   Individual psychology. Some psychologists believe that certain authoritarian or neurotic personality types are predisposed to racist attitudes.

Select what you consider to be the four most important reasons for racism and place them in order of importance, 1 to 4.

Hodder & Stoughton   *© 1994 Paul Higginson. The publishers grant permission for multiple copies of this sheet to be made in the place of purchase for use solely in that institution.*

CASE STUDIES:

NAZI GERMANY

Hitler's Nazi ideology was based on racism. He believed that Germans were a part of an Aryan race (stereotypically tall, blonde and blue-eyed) which was superior to other races. The Jews by contrast were thought of as one of the lowest races. When Hitler came to power their rights and citizenship were removed, they were banned from certain jobs, prohibited from marrying non-Jews, and forced to wear special badges. This led eventually to Hitler's 'Final Solution', the deliberate attempt to exterminate all Jews in the Holocaust. Six million Jews were put to death.

YUGOSLAVIA

With the end of Communism, Yugoslavia (consisting of six republics) began to break up into its traditional ethnic groupings. The largest group, the Serbs, began to grab territory in other republics like Croatia and Bosnia (where substantial numbers of ethnic Serbs lived). In the process they began a system of 'ethnic cleansing'. This consisted of rounding up non-Serbs in concentration camps, driving them out of certain 'Serb areas', and in some instances exterminating whole villages. Most of the 'ethnic cleansing' was directed towards Muslims living in Bosnia.

✪ Further study

Do some historical research on both these case studies - perhaps you have already covered Nazi Germany in history classes. Read the newspapers for information on Yugoslavia.

1 Note down comparisons and contrasts between these two events.

2 Which of the nine causes of racism apply to these two cases?

3 People said The Holocaust could never happen again. Do you agree? Explain your answer.

4 Find out about the revival of Nazism in Germany in the 1990s by newspaper research and by talking to your German teacher.

IMMIGRATION TO BRITAIN

During the 1950s and 1960s many immigrants settled in Britain, primarily from the countries of the New Commonwealth

1 Commonwealth citizens had the right to settle in Britain as a result of the Nationality Act, 1948. This Act reflected the fact that many Commonwealth troops had fought for Britain in the Second World War.

2 There was often a lack of social and economic opportunities in the home countries.

3 Britain encouraged immigrants to meet a chronic shortage of labour in certain key sections of the UK economy (usually low-paid jobs that British workers did not want such as cleaning and transport).

4 Many immigrants, particularly those from the West Indies, identified strongly with Britain (the 'mother country').

5 Some came to the UK to escape persecution (for example, Ugandan Asians escaping from General Amin in the early 1970s).

Hodder & Stoughton   © 1994 Paul Higginson. The publishers grant permission for multiple copies of
this sheet to be made in the place of purchase for use solely in that institution.

IMMIGRATION REFORM

In 1986 the Conservative government introduced new visa restrictions on visitors from India, Pakistan, Bangladesh, Ghana and Nigeria. In 1988 the Immigrant Act removed the automatic right of entry of dependents of people who had settled in the UK before 1973 (no such rights existed for those who had settled after 1973). The 1993 Asylum Act restricted the rights of appeal against Home Office decisions on matters such as visa applications, rights of entry and deportation.

RACE RELATIONS ACT

The 1976 Race Relations Act outlawed all forms of racial discrimination (in employment, housing, education, etc.). The Act also widened the scope of the law to include unintended as well as intended discrimination. Furthermore, 'incitement to racial hatred' was made illegal and the Commission for Racial Equality was established to deal with complaints.

Social Statistics on Racial Disadvantage

	White	West Indian	Asian
Unemployment rate	10%	21%	20%
5 or more GCSEs grades A-C	19%	6%	17%
Housing density (2.5 persons or more per bedroom)	2%	54%	65%

Only six MPs are black (out of 651) and there are no senior black judges or police officers.

❏ Questions

1 What kind of problems might new immigrants to this country have to overcome?

2 Until 1993 Germany had hardly any immigration controls; Britain now has strict limitations. Draw up a table listing the arguments for and against immigration control.

3 Suggest reasons for the different statistics in the table above.

4 'It is easy to change the law; changing people's attitudes is much more difficult.' How do you think it might be possible to change racist attitudes? Brainstorm answers and list them on the board.

Hodder & Stoughton   © 1994 Paul Higginson. The publishers grant permission for multiple copies of this sheet to be made in the place of purchase for use solely in that institution.

ANOTHER EXAMPLE OF POLICE PREJUDICE?
OR ANOTHER EXAMPLE OF YOURS?

Do you see a policeman chasing a criminal? Or a policeman harassing an innocent person? Wrong both times. It's two police officers, one in plain clothes, chasing a third party. And it's a good illustration of why we're looking for more recruits from ethnic minorities.

Photograph by Don McCullin.

During the 1980s there was heavy criticism of some police officers for racist attitudes and prejudice against minorities. The poster above is an attempt by the Metropolitan Police to eliminate racial prejudice within the force by actively recruiting officers from the ethnic minorities.

✪ Further study

1　Make a study of an ethnic group (its history, culture, lifestyle, religious beliefs, etc.).

2　Conduct a survey of attitudes towards race in your school or college.

3　Invite a member of the police force into class to talk about equal opportunities.

4　Examine the concept of integration: should minority groups seek to integrate with the majority group, or should they strive to maintain their independent ethnic lifestyle, culture and language?

Hodder & Stoughton　　*© 1994 Paul Higginson. The publishers grant permission for multiple copies of this sheet to be made in the place of purchase for use solely in that institution.*

Prejudice

Prejudice, from the Latin pre-judicare, means to pre-judge, or to decide before we have examined the facts. Prejudice often leads to discrimination and the belief that another person, who may be different in some way, is also inferior. Although generally associated with race and sex, prejudice exists in many forms and we have probably all encountered it at some time in our lives. Complete the table below with appropriate examples and include in number 14 other types of prejudice not mentioned.

Prejudice based on	Example
1 Age	Companies refusing to interview older workers over 55.
2 Area of abode	'Northerners all wear cloth caps and eat fish and chips!' 'Southerners are all unfriendly snobs!'
3 Type of clothes worn	
4 Social class	
5 Accent	
6 Physical appearance	
7 Intelligence	
8 Sexual orientation	
9 Length of hair	
10 Religion	
11 Occupation (e.g. used car dealer, police officer)	
12 Gender	
13 Race	
14	

Discussion

1 "Discrimination is usually based on generalised ideas which people refuse to change even when confronted with evidence that contradicts their original views." Why are some people unwilling to change their original views?

2 "Prejudiced ideas are often translated into dangerous actions." Give examples from your own experience or from history.

3 "Prejudice and racial tension are part of human nature and will always exist." Do you agree or disagree with this statement (give reasons)?

4 Are jokes based on race or nationality acceptable (for example, Irish jokes)?

Hodder & Stoughton

© *1994 Paul Higginson. The publishers grant permission for multiple copies of this sheet to be made in the place of purchase for use solely in that institution.*

KEY EVENTS IN RECENT HISTORY

1910	The Union of South Africa was created (with a policy of whites-only government).
1936	Blacks lost the vote; Asians and Coloureds could vote - but only for whites (this right was removed in 1956).
1948	Afrikaaner or Nationalist governments introduced apartheid (the 'separate development' of the Africans).
1958	The Bantustans were created - separate regions set aside for blacks; 80 per cent of the population were given 14 per cent of the land.
1962	The UN imposed a trade boycott (sanctions) which was largely ineffective. It was followed later by sporting sanctions. Nelson Mandela is jailed.
1976	Black opposition (demonstrations, strikes, sabotage, etc.) culminated in the Soweto uprising.
1982	The Government now led by PW Botha, introduced small reforms (for example, Asians and Coloureds could vote but the all-white Parliament continued).
1990	FW de Klerk introduces major reforms, lifts the ban on the African National Congress (ANC), releases Nelson Mandela, and promises to dismantle apartheid and create a 'new South Africa'.
1992	There is increasing tension and violence between the two major black groups, the ANC and the Inkatha Movement led by Zulu Chief Buthelezi.
1993	Multi-party talks result in a new constitution and the ending of three centuries of white rule.
1994	South Africans of all races elect their first democratic government.

WHAT APARTHEID MEANT IN PRACTICE

1   All blacks had to carry passes; failure led to imprisonment.

2   Blacks lived in separate housing in segregated reserves.

3   Important jobs were open to whites only.

4   Sexual relations or marriage between white and black was a crime.

5   'Petty apartheid' meant segregated restaurants, beaches, sporting events, swimming pools, toilets, and even separate doors into post offices.

6   Political rights were denied to blacks: they were unable to vote, stand for office, form political parties, go on strike, or join a trade union. They had no freedom of speech or assembly.

Hodder & Stoughton   © *1994 Paul Higginson. The publishers grant permission for multiple copies of this sheet to be made in the place of purchase for use solely in that institution.*

Worksheet 2
Continued

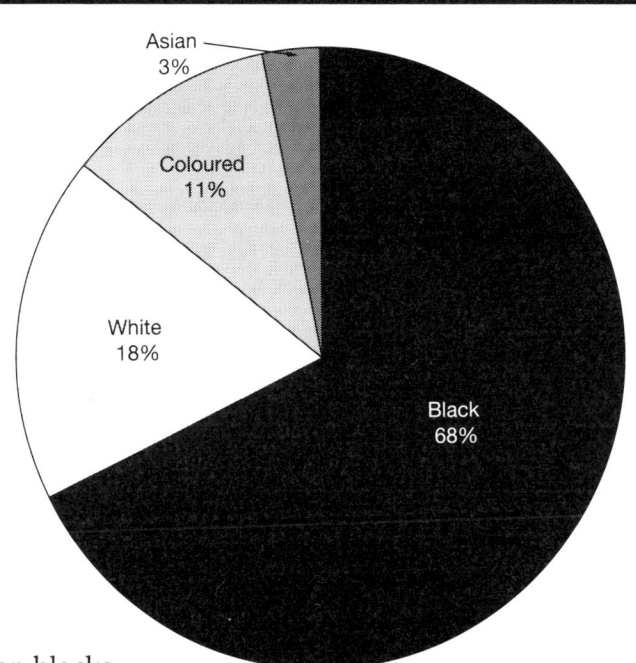

Population of South Africa (1993)

KEY FACTS

1   Whites earn on average four times more than blacks.

2   The pupil:teacher ratio in black schools is double that in white schools.

3   96 per cent of the country's farmland is white owned.

4   The Government spends ten times more on white education than on black.

■ Activities

In groups of three draw up answers to the following questions.

1   Why do you think apartheid was originally introduced, and why was it sustained for so long? Suggest reasons that supporters of apartheid might use to justify its continuation.

2   Why have sanctions been largely ineffective? Draw up a list of arguments for and against the use of sanctions.

3   Why was the implementation of petty apartheid so important, along with the restriction on inter-racial sex and marriage?

4   Archbishop Tutu has said that black majority rule can only be achieved by the use of non-violent methods. Is violence justified in order to bring down a government? Illustrate your answer with examples from other countries (for example, India, Nazi Germany, Ireland, East Germany and Palestine).

5   South Africa is now getting ready for democracy and majority rule. How and why has the change come about?

6   Many white South Africans are bitterly opposed to reform. List the arguments you would use to persuade them to accept free elections and 'one person one vote'.

Hodder & Stoughton   © 1994 Paul Higginson. The publishers grant permission for multiple copies of this sheet to be made in the place of purchase for use solely in that institution.

Racial Discrimination: True or False?

Test your knowledge by writing **T** (True) or **F** (False) next to the following:

 1 More people leave Britain each year than enter.   ----

 2 Ethnic minorities make up 10 per cent of the population.   ----

 3 There are no black Conservative MPs.   ----

 4 At the time of the 1981 Toxteth riots in Liverpool black unemployment was 50 per cent in the area.   ----

 5 The far Right political parties in Britain such as the National Front and the British National Party have 14,000 members.   ----

 6 The Labour Party has consistently refused to allow black sections within the party.   ----

 7 Seven per cent of Afro-Caribbean men have managerial or professional jobs.   ----

 8 There are no black trade union leaders.   ----

 9 By the year 2000 the non-white British population will double.   ----

10 Most black men with degrees have professional jobs.   ----

11 In a recent survey 10 per cent of the population described themselves as racially prejudiced.   ----

12 In 1932 the Nazis won 37 per cent of the vote in democratic German elections, becoming the largest single party.   ----

13 There is no such thing as a 'true Brit' or an ethnic Englishman or woman.   ----

14 Racial discrimination is not illegal.   ----

15 As a percentage of population, more Asians than whites own their own house.   ----

16 Over 1,000 British police officers are black.   ----

17 In some London boroughs and districts in the Midlands, ethnic minorities make up over 50 per cent of the total population.   ----

18 The Irish community in London makes up approximately 17 per cent of the total population of the city.   ----

19 10 per cent of all doctors in the UK were born overseas.   ----

20 Young Asians are just as likely to enter higher education as young whites.   ----

Hodder & Stoughton

© *1994 Paul Higginson. The publishers grant permission for multiple copies of this sheet to be made in the place of purchase for use solely in that institution.*

12 Crime and Punishment

LEVELS OF CRIME

There are many different types of crime, including property and violent crime, white collar crime, opportunist crime and professional crime. Study the following statistics on crime rates and then answer the questions.

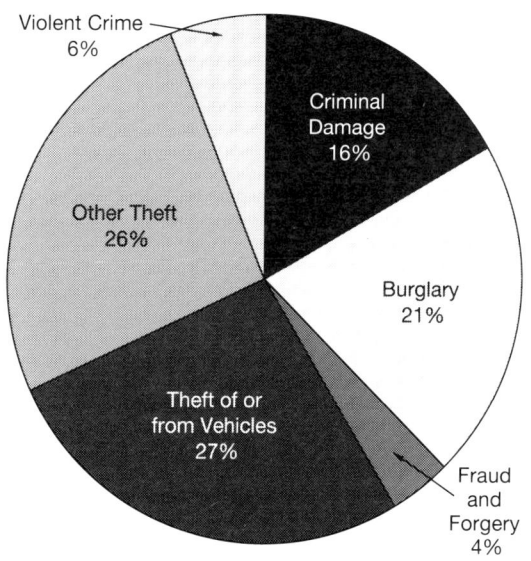

Notifiable offences recorded by the police
(England and Wales), 1992

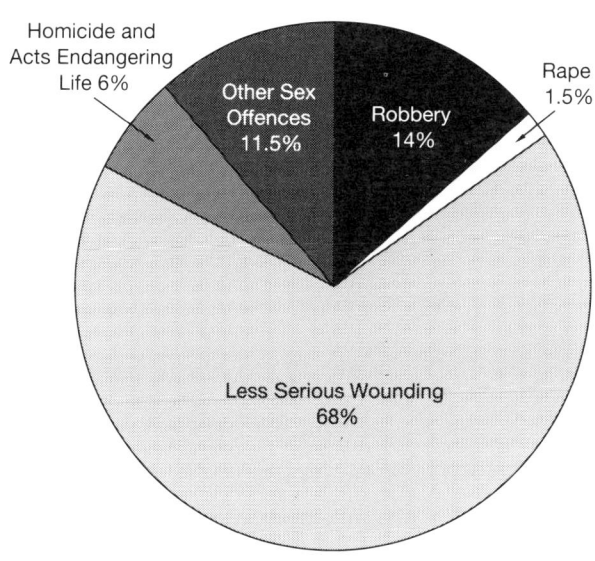

Violent crime, 1992

❑ Questions

1 What percentage of crime is property crime and how much crime is against the person?

2 Criminal damage represented less than 1 per cent of offences in 1957. Suggest reasons for the dramatic increase since then.

3 Car crime has increased from 10 per cent in 1957 to 27 per cent today. What factors may help to explain this increase?

4 'There are great regional and locality variations in crime figures.' Explain this statement.

5 Only about a quarter of all crime is recorded by the police. Suggest reasons for this.

6 The number of rapes reported to the police has trebled in the last ten years - what reasons might there be for such an increase?

7 The increasing number of telephones and the growth of household insurance has dramatically increased police figures for some crimes. Why?

Hodder & Stoughton
© 1994 Paul Higginson. The publishers grant permission for multiple copies of this sheet to be made in the place of purchase for use solely in that institution.

CAUSES OF CRIME

Why do people commit crime? Below are some suggested explanations:

1 Social environment. Unemployment, poor education, poverty, poor housing, impersonal surroundings, lack of a sense of community can all prevent people from feeling a part of society. In some inner-city areas of Britain, crime is seen as normal behaviour.

2 Media. The increase in violence on television and the glamorisation of crime.

3 Declining values. The family as an institution is weakening. There is not enough discipline from parents and schools. There is a decline in religion - people no longer have a strong moral framework for their lives.

4 Society is too soft on criminals. Police, courts, and politicians do not do enough to deter offenders. Crime often pays.

5 Increase in opportunity. As society becomes more affluent, there are more goods to take, cars to steal, etc.

6 Drink and drugs. The majority of assaults occur after heavy alcohol consumption.

7 Young male image seeking. Boredom and a desire to conform to a 'one of the lads' image. Violence and/or acquisition of possessions improves this image and brings status for young, working-class males.

8 Economics. A way of getting rich and acquiring possessions. Some make a career of crime.

9 Genetics. Behaviour is inherited (like a violent temper) from our parents through our genes.

10 Evil exists. Some people are bad, some are good. Bad people commit crime, and need a religious or moral framework to become good.

■ Activities

In groups of three -

1 List the ten causes of crime in order of importance/influence. What do you feel is the main cause of crime?

2 Look at a daily newspaper and try to identify the causes of some of the crimes committed.

3 How important are our genes in determining our behaviour? Why do people brought up in the same family have such different characteristics and patterns of behaviour?

4 Do you feel that your morals are stronger or weaker than those of your parents and grandparents? Have moral standards declined?

Hodder & Stoughton
© 1994 Paul Higginson. The publishers grant permission for multiple copies of this sheet to be made in the place of purchase for use solely in that institution.

PUNISHMENT

There are various methods of dealing with offenders, for example, fines, community service, and imprisonment. It is widely felt that an offender should be punished or made to pay in some way for his or her actions. Below are listed some of the reasons or purposes for the sentences that are imposed.

1 **Deterrence.** A harsh punishment may prevent the offender and others from committing further crimes because of the fear of punishment. Some, however, continue to commit crime in spite of harsh penalties. Occasionally judges will impose a harsh sentence as an example to others (but is this fair?).

2 **Rehabilitation.** Offenders are 'treated', not punished: their behaviour must be changed so that they will not re-offend. Emphasis is on education, reform and counselling.

3 **Retribution.** In other words, those who commit crime should pay for it. Is this society taking revenge (overlooking the complexities of individual offences), or is it simply justice (the punishment fits the crime)? Many argue that some offenders actually want a just sentence to pay off the crime they have committed.

4 **Protection.** People and property are protected by removing the offender from society.

5 **Maintenance of the rule of law.** If law and order are to be maintained, and if people are to respect the law, then offenders must be seen to be punished.

■ Activities

1 What should be the main purpose of sentencing? List the five factors above in order of importance.

2 Study the types of sentences on Worksheet 3 and note down which of the above five purposes relates to each sentence. For example, community service is primarily 2 rehabilitation.

3 'Most punishment is counter-productive and does not work (70 per cent of all released prisoners re-offend). There is usually a reason why people commit crime - this must be tackled. Offenders must be "made whole" by counselling and re-education so that they take responsibility for their actions'. Do you agree with this view?

Hodder & Stoughton
© 1994 Paul Higginson. The publishers grant permission for multiple copies of this sheet to be made in the place of purchase for use solely in that institution.

How Can Crime Be Reduced?

A number of practical steps have been taken in the UK in order to try to reduce the crime rate.

1   Action on inner-city estates. For example, providing better lighting, redesigning buildings to cut burglary and vandalism, removing graffiti, providing activities for young people (summer camp, an alcohol free pub, car maintenance schemes). An example is Bradford Safe City area.

2   Neighbourhood Watch. This aims to bring the police and the local community together in support of crime prevention, and to produce a greater sense of neighbourliness.

3   The theft-proof car. Rover and Vauxhall have already produced prototypes of cars which are very difficult to break into. Car theft accounts for a quarter of all recorded crime.

4   Parental responsibility. Making parents responsible for crimes committed by juveniles under 17 (one quarter of all crime). 7,000 recorded crimes are committed by under-10s ever year.

5   Equal opportunities in the police. Increasing the number of ethnic minorities and women in the police force.

6   Adult Tracking. This is used in the US and now in Yorkshire. Volunteer 'trackers' help an adult offender to adapt to a non-criminal way of life by regular meetings (60 times in the first three months).

7   Reparation Schemes. The victim and the offender meet under the guidance of a mediator in order to show offenders the effects of their crime and help victims to express their feelings and come to terms with what has happened. Often these meetings result in reparation - the offender pays, or helps the victim in some way.

8   Tougher sentences. Since 1988 the courts have been increasing penalties for persistent or violent offenders.

❏ Questions

1   Which of these schemes do you feel might be most successful?

2   Can you think of other ways in which crime might be reduced?

3   Most of the above schemes are expensive (as is keeping someone in prison). Do you feel that more money should be spent on law and order and would you be prepared to pay higher taxes to achieve this?

4   'There is no solution to the problem of ever-rising crime.' Do you agree?

Hodder & Stoughton

© 1994 Paul Higginson. The publishers grant permission for multiple copies of this sheet to be made in the place of purchase for use solely in that institution.

Crime Quiz

TICK THE CORRECT ANSWERS

1 How much recorded crime is violent?

    (a) 22%   (b) 13%   (c) 6%

2 What is the peak age for committing crimes?

    (a) 15   (b) 20   (c) 25

3 How many offenders are under 21 years of age?

    (a) 81%   (b) 69%   (c) 58%

4 How many offenders under 21 years of age are male?

    (a) 94%   (b) 84%   (c) 74%

5 Apart from a couple of small decreases in the 80s, crime has increased steadily every year since the 1950s. How much is this increase per annum?

    (a) 2%   (b) 4%   (c) 6%

6 What is the clear-up rate for homicides?

    (a) 61%   (b) 76%   (c) 96%

7 How many young male offenders (10 to 16 years) who commit offences end up in custody?

    (a) 4%   (b) 11%   (c) 19%

8 Most 10 to 16 year old offenders are cautioned. How many of these re-offend later?

    (a) 75%   (b) 50%   (c) 25%

9 Approximately how many offenders who live in the big cities are unemployed?

    (a) 80%   (b) 60%   (c) 40%

10 Approximately how much does it cost to keep an offender in a secure prison (per week)?

    (a) £200   (b) £350   (c) £500

11 What percentage of 31 year olds have been convicted of an offence (excluding motoring offences) at some time in their lives?

    (a) 6%   (b) 18%   (c) 33%

12 How many 15 to 16 year-olds were reconvicted within two years of leaving custody?

    (a) 80%   (b) 60%   (c) 40%

13 A crime is committed in Britain every

    (a) 10 seconds   (b) minute   (c) 10 minutes.

Hodder & Stoughton
© 1994 Paul Higginson. The publishers grant permission for multiple copies of this sheet to be made in the place of purchase for use solely in that institution.

You Are The Magistrate

There are 30,000 Magistrates (or Justices of the Peace) in the UK, who deal with 97 per cent of all criminal cases. They sit in magistrates' courts, often in benches of three, and are unpaid volunteers with no formal legal training.

In groups of three, study the following cases and reach a decision after discussion and deliberation. Write your decision down but do not discuss with other 'benches' until all have finished.

SPEEDING

All the offenders were caught driving at 50 mph in a 30 mph built-up area. They are all pleading guilty.

Mr A   50 year-old wealthy businessman, who earns £100,000 per annum.

Mrs B   28 year-old single parent, unemployed, on her way to pick up the children from school.

Mr C   18 year-old student, says he was late for class

Mr D   26 year-old van-driver, with three recent previous convictions (9 points on his licence) for the same offence. He would lose his job without a licence - magistrates have the discretion not to disqualify someone if this would cause 'exceptional hardship'.

In October 1992 the government introduced a system of unit fines which meant that magistrates had to take disposable income into account when sentencing, i.e. the better off could be fined more than the poor for the same offence. This new system proved to be very unpopular and the government abolished unit fines in September 1993.

Possible sentences
Fine: Maximum £400; note that any fine imposed should not take more than one year to pay off. Also three automatic penalty points on the driving licence. Once 12 points are reached, disqualification for six months to two years normally takes place.

SHOPLIFTING

All plead guilty to stealing a small number of clothes from a local fashion shop.

Mrs F   45 year-old compulsive stealer, with a complicated psychiatric history, and three previous convictions for same offence. She is not poor and does not need the goods she steals; she says she can't stop herself.

Mr G   18 year-old sixth former; his first offence, he says 'he did it for a bet'.

Mr H   32 year-old unemployed family man on a low income. He stole clothes for his children.

Mr J   28 year-old schoolteacher. He stole a Filofax - says it was 'a moment of madness, which he deeply regrets'.

Hodder & Stoughton

© 1994 Paul Higginson. The publishers grant permission for multiple copies of this sheet to be made in the place of purchase for use solely in that institution.

Possible sentences

Fine: Maximum anything up to £2,000 and/or up to six months' imprisonment. Probation order (from 4 months to three years). Community service. Conditional discharge (one or two years, no sentence is imposed but if a further offence is committed within the time period then you are sentenced for the initial offence as well as the further offence).

PUB FIGHT

Three men plead guilty to causing actual bodily harm. They beat up a man in a pub in an argument over a game of pool. The man's injuries include a broken rib and severe bruising and stitches under the eye.

Mr X   21 year old, unemployed, has never worked. He has numerous previous convictions for similar offences. He started the fight - kicked the man in the ribs and stomach. Sober.

Mr Y   30 year old. He has been in and out of work. He has no previous convictions. he kicked the man in the head, causing the damage to his eye. He had drunk a couple of pints.

Mr Z   18 year-old student. Has no previous convictions. He was very drunk. he punched the man twice but then stopped.

Possible sentences

Imprisonment up to six months. Community Service. Fine. Can also award a compensation order, maximum £2,000, to be paid by the offender to victim. This is generally not given with a long prison sentence unless the offender has a large amount of savings as it would be difficult to pay whilst the offender was in prison and therefore not in work.

When you have all reached your decisions, compare them with those of the other benches.

1 Why were your sentences so different?

2 What was the purpose of your sentences? to deter, to punish, to rehabilitate, to protect the public, to set an example?

3 Do you agree with unit fines? Should two people committing exactly the same offence get different fines because they have different income levels?

4 Should the fact that someone had been drinking reduce the severity of the sentence?

Hodder & Stoughton

© *1994 Paul Higginson. The publishers grant permission for multiple copies of this sheet to be made in the place of purchase for use solely in that institution.*

Dealing with Offenders

Below are listed various ways of dealing with offenders. Fill in the gaps in the worksheet outlining the pros and cons of each type of sentence.

Type of Sentence	Pros	Cons
Community service - a number of hours of imposed work helping the community, e.g. cleaning up litter, building an adventure playground. Often used for burglary.		Often seen as a soft option by criminals and the general public. Does not deter?
Probation - the offender is set free but has to keep in regular contact with a probation officer. Most often used for theft or dishonest handling.	Probation officers are able to help and counsel so that re-offending does not occur. It is inexpensive. It prevents overcrowding in the prison system.	
Imprisonment.		
Corporal punishment, e.g. birch or lashing (in some Islamic countries).		
Attendance centre. Young offenders under 21 are often compelled to attend for two-hour sessions on a Saturday.		
Tagging. An electronic bracelet is worn on the ankle or wrist. Conditions are imposed e.g. offender must stay at home from 6 pm to 6 am.		
Fine (paid to court) or compensation (paid to victim).		
Alcohol education programme. Offenders with a drink problem must attend a course at a day centre.		
Capital Punishment: death penalty. Used in many countries (not in UK) for serious crimes.		

Hodder & Stoughton

© 1994 Paul Higginson. The publishers grant permission for multiple copies of this sheet to be made in the place of purchase for use solely in that institution.

Additional Information

USEFUL ADDRESSES

Amnesty International, 1 Easton Street, London, WC1X 8DJ.

British Law Society, Law Society's Hall, Chancery Lane, London WC2A.

Citizenship Foundation, 63 Charterhouse Street, London EC1M 6HJ.

Commission for Racial Equality, Elliot House, 10-12 Allington St., London SW1E 5EM.

Confederation of British Industry, Centre Point, New Oxford Street, London WC1.

Conservative Central Office, 32 Smith Square, London SW1.

Council for Education in World Citizenship, Seymour Mews House, Seymour Mews, London W1H 9PE. A non-partisan educational charity publishing useful broadsheets.

Equal Opportunities Commission (UK), Overseas House, Quay Street, Manchester 3.

The European Parliament Information Office, 8 Storey's Gate, London SW1P 3AT. Publishes free literature for schools.

The Foreign Office has published a useful booklet *Britain in Europe, a guide to 1992, Maastricht and the EC*. Free copies can be obtained from Freepost, PO Box 1992, Burgess Hill, West Sussex, RH15 8QY or call free on 0800 778866.

Greenpeace, 30 Islington Green, London W1.

Help the Aged, 318 St Pauls Road, London N1.

House of Commons Education Unit, Room 507, Norman Shaw Building, Victoria Embankment, London SW1A 2HZ. Publishes a range of free education sheets on every aspect of parliament and government. Organises autumn tours of Parliament for schools (apply in April).

Labour Party, 150 Walworth Road, London SE12.

Liberal Democrats, 4 Cowley Street, London SW1P 3NB.

Low Pay Unit, 9 Poland Street, London W1.

The Magistrates' Association Schools Project. Organises simulations in schools and colleges. Write to your local Justices' Clerks Office or contact your local magistrates' court.

Metropolitan Police Directorate of Public Affairs, New Scotland Yard, London SW1H 08G

National Association for the Care and Resettlement of Offenders (NACRO), 169 Clapham Road, London SW9 0PU.

National Council for Civil Liberties (Women's Rights Unit), 21 Tabard Street, London SE1.

National Union of Students, 461 Holloway Road, London N7.

Plaid Cymru, 51 Cathedral Road, Cardiff CF1 9HD.

The Politics Association, 16 Gower Street, London WC1E 6DP.

Hodder & Stoughton   © 1994 Paul Higginson. The publishers grant permission for multiple copies of this sheet to be made in the place of purchase for use solely in that institution.

The **Politics Association Resource Centre** (PARC), Studio 16, I-Mex Business Park; Hamilton Road, Longsight, Manchester M13 0PD. Books, pamphlets, worksheets, teaching aids, videos on every conceivable topic.

Scottish National Party, 6 Charlotte Street, Edinburgh EH2 4JH. Shelter, 157 Waterloo Road, London SE1 8XF.

Transport and General Workers' Union, Transport House, South Square, London SW1.

UK Office of the European Parliament, 2 Queen Anne's Gate, London SW1H 9AA. Publishes free education packs on Europe. Tel: 071-222 0411

FURTHER READING

Bowes A, Gleeson D and Smith P, *Sociology A Modular Approach*, Oxford University Press.

Cooper P, *Sociology An Introductory Course*, Longman.

Coxall B and Robins L, *Contemporary British Politics*, Macmillan.

Denscombe M, *Sociology Update*, published annually, 32 Shirley Road, Stoneygate, Leicester LE2 3LJ.

Glasgow University Media Group, *More Bad News*, Routledge.

Glasgow University Media Group, *Really Bad News*, Routledge.

Grant W, *Pressure Groups, Politics and Democracy in Britain*, Philip Allan.

Griffith JAG, *The Politics of the Judiciary*, Fontana.

Jones B and Kavanagh D, *British Politics Today*, Manchester University Press.

Jones B (ed), *Political Issues in Britain Today*, Manchester University Press.

Jones B et al, *Politics UK*, Philip Alan.

Joseph M, *Sociology for Everyone*, Polity Press.

Kingdom J, *Government and Politics in Britain*, Polity Press.

Politics Review and *Sociology Review*, published four times per annum, Philip Allan Publishers, Market Place, Deddington, Oxford OX15 0SE.

Pye K and Yates R, *British Politics Ideas & Concepts*, Thornes.

Roberts D, *Politics A New Approach*, Causeway Press.

Robins L, *Politics Pal* and *The Political Update*, inexpensive updates on political events, published annually, 46 The Fairway, Oadby, Leicestershire LE2 2HJ.

Skellington R, *Race in Britain Today*, Sage.

Talking Politics, Journal of the Politics Association.

Keep in touch with current events by reading the quality newspapers, and journals such as *The Economist, New Internationalist, Time* and *Newsweek*.

Hodder & Stoughton   © *1994 Paul Higginson. The publishers grant permission for multiple copies of this sheet to be made in the place of purchase for use solely in that institution.*

ACTIVITIES

1 Visit Parliament (the Commons and/or the Lords) to hear a debate. Either write to your MP for a ticket for Question Time or just turn up and queue. Phone 071-219 4503 to find out if the House is sitting.

2 Visit your local magistrates' court or Crown Court to see the legal system in operation. Telephone in advance to find out a suitable time. If you live near London visit the Old Bailey (071-248 3277).

3 Attend a meeting of your local council. Telephone the town hall or civic centre for details of the next meeting.

4 Arrange a visit to your local police station, or get the local Schools Liaison Officer to come to your college to talk about the role of the police.

5 The Stock Exchange organises tours for school groups. Phone 071 588 2355.

6 The Liberal Democrats organise an annual Youth and Student Day at Westminster each February with debates, MPs' Question Time and Policy Workshops. Inexpensive, non-partisan and very stimulating. Phone 071-222 7998 in the November of the preceding year.

7 Most pressure groups (CND, Greenpeace, Amnesty, etc.) will send speakers to schools and colleges to take part in debates and discussions.

8 Invite your local councillor or MP to take part in a question and answer session.

9 Organise a Europe Day in your college with workshops on United Europe - For and Against, and Career Opportunities in Europe; hold European Language Taster sessions (language teachers give short introductions to a particular country's language, culture and history).

10 Hold a mock election with student candidates, hustings, election manifestos, and video party political broadcasts.

GENERAL STUDIES PAST PAPER ESSAY QUESTIONS

The following essay questions have been selected from a typical range of past papers.

1 Does 'the working class' still exist in the United Kingdom? (Oxford 1990)

2 Discuss the methods of raising money, apart from direct taxation, that are available to central and local government. Include in your discussion the advantages and disadvantages of the Community Charge (Poll Tax). (NEAB 1990)

3 Outline the main reasons for the rapid growth of immigration into Britain in the 1950s and 1960s. Discuss the tensions that this has created in British society. (AEB 1992)

4 Should limits be placed, in your view, on 'the freedom of reporters to go about their jobs'? (AEB 1992)

5 Comment briefly on four of the following: (a) Question Time in the House of Commons; (b) 'the letter of the law'; (c) 'merger mania'; (d) 'equal pay for equal work'; (e) 'honesty is the best policy'; (f) social minorities. (Oxford 1990)

6 Discuss the events leading up to and the likely consequences of one of the following: the reunification of Germany, the current economic strength of Japan, the recent changes in South Africa, the introduction of the single European Market in 1992. (NEAB 1991)

Hodder & Stoughton   © 1994 Paul Higginson. The publishers grant permission for multiple copies of this sheet to be made in the place of purchase for use solely in that institution.

7 Discuss the claim that the British parliamentary system is both unfair and undemocratic. (NEAB 1992)

8 Is there a case for setting strict controls on the sentences, costs and damages imposed by judges, magistrates and juries? (Oxford 1991)

9 Friends of the Earth, the Green Party and Greenpeace are examples of organisations seeking to protect the environment. Discuss the differing methods they have used and the extent to which they have been successful in their aims. (AEB 1992)

10 There has been much discussion in recent years over the issue of the ordination of women as priests. Outline the arguments put forward by the opposing sides in this debate and come to a considered conclusion. (AEB 1990)

11 'Britain's best hope for the future is to be part of a federal Europe.' Examine this statement. (Oxford 1993)

12 What might be the economic and social implications of a reduction in the standard rate of income tax? (AEB 1993)

13 What factors may influence the way people vote in a general election? Oxford 1993

14 'We are all equal under the law.' How far is this assertion true in England and Wales today? (Oxford 1993)

15 Discuss the reasons why people permanently leave the country of their birth. Illustrate your answer by referring to population movements in the twentieth century. (AEB 1993)

16 Can pressure groups have a greater influence on government policy than civil servants or Members of Parliament? (Oxford 1993)

17 Should a given minimum proportion of specific jobs and occupations be allocated to those belonging to ethnic minorities? (Oxford 1993)

18 What do you understand by the term 'stereotype'? To what extent doe stereotypes of race, gender and class affect attitudes and behaviour in the world today? (NEAB 1993)

Hodder & Stoughton   © 1994 Paul Higginson. The publishers grant permission for multiple copies of this sheet to be made in the place of purchase for use solely in that institution.